Glennyce Eckersley is an international angel expert and the author of many successful books, including *An Angel at My Shoulder* and *Saved by the Angels*. Her work has been widely featured in the media and she is the resident expert on a Sky *Real Lives* series dedicated to angels. She gives talks and runs angel workshops around the world and lives in Manchester.

An
Angel
to Guide Me

*How Angels Speak to Us
from the Beyond*

Glennyce Eckersley

RIDER

LONDON · SYDNEY · AUCKLAND · JOHANNESBURG

3 5 7 9 10 8 6 4 2

First published in 2009 by Rider, an imprint of Ebury Publishing

Ebury Publishing is a Random House Group company

The Random House Group Limited Reg. No. 954009

Addresses for companies within the Random House Group can be found at www.rbooks.co.uk

A CIP catalogue record for this book is available from the British Library

The Random House Group Limited supports The Forest Stewardship Council (FSC), the leading international forest certification organisation. All our titles that are printed on Greenpeace approved FSC certified paper carry the FSC logo. Our paper procurement policy can be found at www.rbooks.co.uk/environment

Printed and bound in Great Britain by Cox and Wyman Ltd, Reading, Berkshire

ISBN 978-1-8460-4160-0

Copies are available at special rates for bulk orders. Contact the sales development team on 020 7840 8487 or visit www.booksforpromotions.co.uk for more information

To buy books by your favourite authors and register for offers visit www.rbooks.co.uk

To Matilda,
my dearest granddaughter,
with much love

CONTENTS

ACKNOWLEDGEMENTS

I would like to thank most sincerely the following people for their encouragement, support and love, making the writing of this book possible. A huge vote of thanks to Judith Kendra, Publishing Director of Rider Books, for her years of faith in me and her words of inspiration. To Sue Lascelles, my editor, thank you for your infinite patience, kindness and wisdom. To my family, Ross, Rachel and Ed, Gill and Mike and, of course, Matilda, to whom this book is dedicated. To Kathryn Flett, *Observer* columnist and broadcaster, for her kindness. To my friends, always ready to listen and help with research: Rev Gillian Gordon, Greta Woolf, Mary Bullough, Julie Fearnhead, Susan Cahal, Sue James, Patsy Allan, Pam and Roy Cuthbert and Lynne Readett. I would also like to offer my thanks to Richard Lyons, Howard Casofsky and Alison Levesley and the staff of Gorton Monastery.

Finally, sincere gratitude and thanks go to the contributors for their generosity and kindness in allowing me to include their very personal stories. They are: Margaret Adams, Sandra Atkins, Kath Bann, Linda Bolton, Joan Bullock, Paula Carter, Laura Davis, Anna Dawson, Pamela Derbyshire, Lesley Easton, Francis Ellington, Richard Evans, Julie Fearnhead, Beryl Felstead, Tracey Fisher, Joanne Glover, Rose Hall, Sylvia Heathcote, Robert Heaton, Deena Kearney, Heather Kendrick, Trevor Lawrence, Faye Lorenze, Diane Marsh, Rose Mason, Sheena Mary Moyes, Polly Parker, Verity Pembroke, Roswitha Pfennich, Sue

Robinson, Edith Rowbothom, Dr Peter Ruppel, Sarah Stefan Sirkorski, Claire Smith, Clarice Smith, Brian Spencer, Connie Swift, Penny Taylor, Rosemary Thompson, Amanda Watkins, Veronica Williams, Beccy Wood, Gaye Young and Jane Zoretti.

How Can the Angels Reach Us?

*I*n today's hectic world, the angels have to struggle through a blizzard of technology to reach us. Mobile phones, computers, DVD players and gadgetry can create technological snowstorms, blinding our senses when it comes to an awareness of these magical beings. The background chatter of our busy lives may also mean that we no longer hear what they are trying to tell us, and that we unwittingly block the subtle messages and symbols that they send to us. These angel signs and symbols appear constantly in our lives, yet all too often we fail to recognise them. However, it's never too late to heal the connection.

We may simply need to give ourselves permission to take a little time out. When we are able to enjoy some time to ourselves, we can begin to concentrate on the spiritual aspects of life. Take a moment now to ask yourself how long it is, for instance, since you last sat for an hour, nursing a cup of coffee and gazing through the window, collecting your thoughts. Yet if you had done so, you might well have seen a flurry of butterflies that symbolised someone special, or a robin bringing an angel message meant for you...

If we can only give ourselves the gift of a few minutes' peace and quiet away from the daily grind, we might be surprised by what those moments bring us. Music that holds a special significance for us could come to mind, or a special fragrance might waft through the room. Memories of a taste might surface, transporting us back to childhood or to an important celebration, when we were surrounded by those we loved. These different types of sensation are all angelic messages and once we start to become aware of them we might be surprised by how many come our way – and also how much comfort they can offer. And comfort is certainly something that we all need in today's uncertain world.

From time immemorial people have looked to the angels for reassurance and guidance. During wars, natural disasters, epidemics and economic crises, there have been documented resurgences of angelic interest. In fact, if we only look back as far as the past hundred years, we will see that towards the end of the twentieth century angels once more featured prominently in films, writing and art. After decades that saw phenomenal advances in science and technology, giving rise to unprecedented materialism (in the West at least), we reached a point where many of us had all the material goods we would ever need – but still happiness eluded us. And so we turned once more to the angels.

In this new millennium, our fear of the unknown and our unease about the future remain as strong as ever. Worrying trends connected to global natural stability and, in more recent times, economic catastrophe have once more seen people turn to the angels in large numbers. Could these worrying situations in fact be wake-up calls? Are we being shown that happiness does not lie with material or financial gain? Perhaps that's the truth, but one thing is clear: we need help to find our way. Perhaps now more than ever, we need comfort and guidance from an otherworldly source.

Luckily for us, the angels are there for us whenever we are ready to receive them. This book will explain how the angels communicate with us through the five physical senses of sight, hearing, smell, taste and touch, as well as through the mysterious sixth sense. Each chapter will explore how one of these qualities, such as sight or sound, acts as a gateway through which the angels can connect with us.

Amazing true stories reveal how people from all around the world have had angelic experiences that appear to have been tailor-made for them, speaking specifically to them in the ways they recognise and understand the best. For instance, as these stories show, someone who is hard of hearing is less likely to appreciate heavenly music so an angelic intervention in the form of a vision is more appropriate for that person. Similarly, a chef in a busy restaurant is unlikely to single out a heavenly fragrance among all the different kitchen smells so an angelic encounter in the form of touch would be more appropriate for her. Likewise, nature lovers seem to be particularly attuned to noticing angelic signs in the landscape, whereas a painter might see angel colours.

Angelic experiences appear to be 'bespoke', by which I mean that we are each contacted by angels in the ways that are most suitable for our personalities, our circumstances and what we can cope with. The appearance of a full-blown angel, dressed in white and with wings, is a rare event which my research suggests usually only happens in the most dramatic situations.

Finally, the chapter dedicated to the sixth sense explores the phenomenon of intuition – the sense of inner knowing that guides us in certain directions and to certain people. It will show us how we can encourage and enhance the sixth sense in relation to our daily lives. The concept of the inner angel is explained here.

By helping you to become aware of the angelic presences that surround you, *An Angel to Guide Me* aims to give you a little more insight into how to help yourself in your own life, whatever your needs or aspirations. Whenever you choose to search for inner peace, you can be sure that the angels will show you the way. What is more, they will do so in the ways that suit you best.

Communication with angels starts when you recognise they are there.

MURRAY STEINMAN

CHAPTER 1

Visions of Angels

S ight seems to command an authority all of its own. Whereas our other senses often seem to be open to interpretation – for instance, we may ask ourselves, 'Was that fragrance *really* from another world?', 'Did I actually *hear* heavenly music?' – the power of sight literally shapes the way we view the world and the old adage 'seeing is believing' holds true for many of us. Sight in the form of a vision can literally stop us in our tracks and profoundly challenge our perspectives on life.

Perhaps the most dramatic sight of all is that of an angel. As the stories in this chapter show, such a vision is without doubt a life-changing event, never forgotten by those who have been lucky enough to experience it.

An Angel in the Alps

An angel came to Penny's rescue one summer in the French Alps. Keen to explore and climb higher than she had ever done before, Penny had accepted an invitation to accompany a group of friends on a climbing holiday.

It had been a wonderful experience so far, but in truth a little harder going than Penny had anticipated. The main group was a good deal more experienced than her and she found the climbing very challenging at times. On the fourth day she was feeling rather weak and struggled a little, but said nothing to her friends; she desperately didn't want to spoil the holiday for the others.

Misfortune struck late morning as Penny, feeling a little wobbly, over-reached and suddenly slipped. Plunging downwards, she felt sheer terror grip her even though she knew she was firmly roped to her friend. She seemed to fall forever before she crash-landed onto a ledge below. Above her, her friend had slipped too, but she had managed to halt her fall by gripping onto a large rock before scrabbling to safety.

It was immediately obvious that Penny was badly injured and that pulling her up from the ledge was not an option. Her friends phoned for help, but there was no way of telling just how long she would have to wait for the emergency services to arrive or how they would reach her when they did.

Frightened and fighting panic, she lay on her small ledge. Her pain became increasingly intense, and she wondered just what the extent of her injuries would be. Inevitably the worst possible scenarios rushed through her thoughts.

At that moment, a warm shaft of sunlight landed on Penny's face – or so she thought at first – as she turned her face away from the rock. Although the day was bright, the sun was well hidden behind the clouds and the intensely bright light was certainly not from sunshine. The warmth and light washed over her, taking her pain with it.

In the centre of this light, Penny made out a face, beautiful and smiling and very clear. It brought a sensation of calm and confidence. Incredible though it seemed to Penny, she was in no doubt that this was an angel sent to calm her. The angel was with Penny for only a moment, but she knew instinctively that she would be rescued and that all would be well.

Although it took a long time for the rescue teams to reach Penny, the feeling of calm and peace stayed with her the whole time. Despite a badly broken leg and wrist, she experienced no more pain, even when being lifted onto a stretcher.

Telling me her story, Penny says, 'I was definitely not hallucinating. The pain was keeping me sharply focused and I knew instantly that this was an angel.'

Always close to her grandmother, who had passed away some time before, Penny feels that this lady was instrumental in helping her. Although it was not the face of her grandmother in that bright light, she feels sure her grandmother sent the angel when Penny needed one most. It was a wonderful sight that quite literally saved and changed Penny's life.

*Be not afraid but let your world be
lit by miracles.*

A COURSE IN MIRACLES

An Angel Book

As well as the powerful testimonies of people who have seen incredible heavenly visions, throughout this book you will find some simple exercises to encourage light to enter into your own life. You might find it helpful to keep a special 'Angel Book' in which you can jot down your responses to the exercises, and also make a note of any angelic signs that appear in your own life. You can use it to record the way you feel after working with the affirmations and meditations that you will find in these pages.

The simple affirmations in this book will help you to focus on what you really wish to see come true in the future, and the meditations will help you nurture your belief in angels, encouraging their presence in your daily routine.

To work with an affirmation, memorise it and then repeat it quietly to yourself now and again throughout the day. Here is a good one to begin with.

~ AFFIRMATION ~

*Today, I see beauty in the world
all around me.*

See Your Angel of Light

Although we may not all be lucky enough to see an angel in our own lifetime (to be honest, my research over the years suggests that such an experience is pretty rare), we can nevertheless open our minds to the fact that there are signs and symbols all around us that confirm the presence of angels in our lives.

The angels are present in our lives because they love us and believe we are worthy of their love. If we consciously look for angelic signs and then reflect on them, this will nurture our sense of being guided by the angels and help us to build up our own sense of self-belief. In the long term, a sense of self-belief supported by the angels can lead to a positive and enriching path in life.

The following simple meditation will help you to see in your mind's eye how powerful the angel presence in your own life is already. Read the meditation all the way through before you begin to familiarise yourself with it.

Choose a comfortable spot in the house at a time when you can be alone and quiet. Sitting still, slow your breathing. Once you feel calm, you may wish to light a candle on which to concentrate, or simply close your eyes. Be aware of your breath entering and leaving your body as you relax into your seat.

Picture yourself at the head of a lush, green valley with a little path stretching out in front of you. Slowly, walk down the path into the valley floor, noticing the sound of birdsong and the gentle rustle of the breeze. Soon the path leads into a wooded area where the trees allow light and sunshine to filter through in a dappled pattern. The air is warm, and you feel comfortable and safe.

You reach a gate on the path, which opens easily when you give it a little push. Step through and you will see you have entered a clearing, in the middle of which is a stone-circled well. Approach the well and you will see it is not a deep dark bottomless well but a shallow sparkling ring of water, reflecting the sunlight and raising your spirits. Let your fingers dip into the water and be aware that this is a life-giving element.

Looking up from the well, you are aware of a figure standing on the opposite side and at once you recognise this as your angel. Light shines from the beautiful face as the angel stretches out a hand towards you. What do you see in the open hand?

This is a gift you specifically need at this time in your life. It may represent a quality such as love, courage or self-belief; whatever it is, you know exactly what it is you long for. Accept the gift and thank the angel as she slowly fades, leaving you feeling positive and refreshed.

Slowly retrace your steps, through the clearing and the gate and down the little path to your starting point. As you gradually become aware again of your own room, realise that you have the angel's blessing and gift with you – and that they will never fade.

For, without being seen, angels are present
around us.

St Francis de Sales

See the Angels at Hand

Few of us, hopefully, will find ourselves stranded in the Alps or in need of rescue, but we all need angels in our lives. We must look for signs of them, which can be subtle at times, but which are there for us all to see if we look with fresh eyes.

Complete the simple following exercise and answer the questions as truthfully as you can. Write your answers down in your Angel Book and return to them from time to time to see how much they change during the course of a few weeks.

* When did you last evaluate your priorities?

* What are the four top priorities in your life?

* Do you allow yourself quality 'alone time' each week?

* What qualities would you wish to increase in your life?

* How long is it since you counted your blessings?

* You are a loving person, worthy of love. List the reasons why.

Reflecting on your answers, consider what they mean to you and how they might relate to the presence of angels in your life.

Angel Smiles

At some point in our lives we will all face a challenge – of that there can be no doubt. For some people the challenge will be greater than most: certainly Pamela felt her inner resources had been stretched to the limit. Being treated for breast cancer over the course of several months had tested her, but she felt blessed by her strong faith and the wonderful care and concern she had received from family and friends. She now faced a check-up to find out if all was clear or, worryingly, if further treatment would be necessary. The night before her appointment, Pamela found sleep impossible. Sitting up in bed, she wondered if she should give up on the idea of sleep altogether and go downstairs to have a cup of tea or read for a while. Her mind was in turmoil as she stared into the darkness.

Suddenly, a figure appeared at the foot of the bed, smiling at Pamela with a wonderfully happy face. Pamela stared in disbelief at the figure of a very beautiful young man. There was a glow around him. When he faded as quickly as he had appeared, Pamela was left with the amazing sensation that this had, in fact, been an angelic presence.

The all-important check-up the following day brought the best news possible, confirming that she was in fact in the clear and that no further treatment would be necessary. Pamela's sense of relief was overwhelming. As she drove away from the hospital, the vision of the angel came into her thoughts and she knew for certain that he had been telling her all would be well.

Two years later, Pamela found herself with the enjoyable but stressful task of helping to arrange her son's wedding. Logistically it was a challenge: the guests had to travel to a rather isolated location and should the weather be wet – and this was the UK in summer, remember! – the whole day might be ruined. The night before the big day Pamela lay awake in her hotel room, worrying about the celebrations the next morning. So much planning had gone into this event and she very much wanted the day to be perfect, especially as it was the wedding of her only child.

To her astonishment, a glow appeared in the darkness of the bedroom. Standing before her once more was the same beautiful figure – the same angel who had appeared before her hospital appointment. Once more he gazed at Pamela with the most wonderful smile. As the figure vanished, she knew for certain this time that all would be well.

The day turned out to be perfection itself: in spite of it being the wettest summer on record, they enjoyed warm sunshine. Every aspect of the day was wonderful, exceeding everyone's expectations. Pamela felt so blessed and grateful to her beautiful angel for his reassurance and love.

The angels in high places who minister to us reflect God's smile; their faces are luminous.

ROBERT GILBERT WALSH

* ✳ *

Truly it is in the darkness that one finds the light, so when we are in sorrow, then this light is nearest of all to us.

MEISTER ECKHART

Peace

The sun streamed down through the beautiful windows of Gorton Monastery as I prepared for my workshop.

Close to the inner city of Manchester, Gorton Monastery is an amazing building which has been described as one of the city's hidden treasures, and even as a northern Taj Mahal! Built by half a dozen Franciscan monks, this truly awesome building was designed by the famous architect Edward Welby Pugin. In the latter part of the twentieth century, it began to fall into disrepair and became prey to vandalism. Happily, after many years of fund-raising (and also receiving some grants), it recently reopened its doors and has been restored very nearly to its former glory.

No longer a consecrated building, it holds many events of a secular nature. However, there are also many spiritual activities organised by the building's Spiritual Director, Alison Levesley. In fact, the spiritual atmosphere in the place today is amazing. The building is literally full of angels, fashioned from stone and from flesh and blood! Interestingly, the monks built the monastery on a spot where several ley lines converge. It provides a stunning setting for workshops and has lost none of its original sacred atmosphere.

So there I was, arranging the room and waiting for people to arrive, with a feeling of happy anticipation. It came as little surprise that the day produced some very special events and stories.

Everyone who came through the door of the workshop room that morning was smiling and I don't think it was simply because of the sunshine. One lady found a white feather floating through a window and announced that the angels were already waiting for us! I noticed another lady arrive with an eager expression on her face. Tall and dark, this was Polly, who had a very special story to tell and happily agreed that I might share it with you.

The story concerns Polly's grandmother, who was involved in a very sad yet inspiring sequence of events during the First World War. As if the war was not enough to contend with, a dreadful flu epidemic was sweeping across Europe and many people died as a result. Polly's grandmother had two daughters, Alice and Annie, much loved and dear to all the family. Alice was only eighteen years old when she complained of feeling very unwell one morning. Retiring to bed with flu symptoms, she didn't survive the night, so swiftly did the illness overcome her .To add to the heartbreak, Annie also died soon afterwards from the same dreadful sickness, leaving their mother inconsolable.

Months passed, and Polly's grandmother found each day a struggle. Weighed down with grief, she tried hard to complete each day's chores. One morning in her dining room, she was amazed to see a bright figure begin to emerge in a dark corner of the room. Surrounded by light, the figure was incredibly beautiful. A profound accompanying sensation of love made her realise this was an angel.

Staring at the figure in wonder, Polly's grandmother then saw the most amazing sight. Slowly the angel lifted one huge, white wing to reveal both her daughters sheltered beneath! As this wonderful vision faded, the feeling of peace she had longed for engulfed her – the overwhelming joy of knowing that her daughters were in the care of an angel would carry her though her grief.

*In times of great sadness, Angels bring
comfort and peace to loved ones.*

A CALENDAR OF ANGELS

* * *

*Their garments are white, but with an
unearthly whiteness. I cannot describe it,
for it cannot be compared to earthly
whiteness; it is much softer to the eye.
These bright angels are enveloped in a light
so different from ours that by comparison
everything else seems dark. When you see a
band of fifty you are lost in amazement.
They seem like golden plates, constantly
moving like so many suns.*

PÈRE LAMY

A Path to Peace

What would happen if the tasks you tell yourself must be done
today were simply not completed? Would the world stop
turning? I think not.

Make a decision to leave non-essential chores undone and
relax instead...

✳ Evaluate the really important things in your life and thank God and his angels for them.

✳ Make a weekly plan, scheduling time for the people and activities that give you the greatest happiness. Life is too short to keep putting off people so you can do the dusting!

✳ Break your routine: go somewhere you keep promising yourself you'll visit but never get around to.

✳ Buy a book written by a favourite author and treat yourself to an afternoon reading with your feet up.

✳ Visit your nearest cathedral or church and soak in the atmosphere of all the people who have gone before, who are now with the angels. Promise yourself that you will make the most of your time on earth and enjoy the life you have.

✳ Most importantly, lighten up and have a laugh with your friends: laughter really is the best medicine.

✳ ✳ ✳

Loosen up. You are never too old, too professional, or too accomplished to laugh and be silly. Allow yourself to play. Let your inner child out and enjoy your life.

TAVIS SMILEY

*You are never given a wish without also being
given the power to make it come true.*

RICHARD BACH

Ray of Light

The scientist Sir Isaac Newton (1642–1727) famously discovered that, although sunlight appears to be white, it is really a blend of colours. He performed a series of experiments in which he guided a shaft of sunlight through a glass prism in a darkened room so that the white light separated into its seven constituent colours – the colours of the rainbow. This was obviously of great scientific interest, and colour is now also central to a variety of healing therapies. We are all aware of the benefits of infrared and ultraviolet light.

A light wave is measured in three ways: wavelength, frequency and amplitude. A wave with a short wavelength has a high frequency and a great deal of energy. Amplitude is related to the brightness of the wave and gives a measure of its intensity.

The entire universe is bathed in such energy waves: cosmic rays, gamma rays, X-rays, radio waves – to name but a few. Keeping this in mind, could it be that the light from angels (which many believe are beings of pure energy) surrounds us at all times but only becomes visible when their wavelength is adjusted to suit the human eye? Do the angels, in effect, surround us at all times like radio waves?

Just as we cannot hear the radio until we switch it on, so we cannot see the angels until we find ourselves in the right emotional channel. A sort of emotional tuning-in often seems to happen during treatments that have a spiritual element, such as reiki. (Indeed, several stories in this book appear to confirm this theory.)

Similarly, bereaved people also often find they are in a certain mental and emotional 'zone', which allows the angels to come through. Often, the appearance of angels takes the form of light and appears to transport the grieving person from the depths of sadness to elation and real hope. Certainly this was the case for Kath, a close friend of mine, who is willing to share her experience.

True friendship is a knot that angel hands have tied.

ANON

The Light of Love

Losing someone you love is never easy; there is no magical formula that can make the pain go away. Loved ones can leave us in many different ways – suddenly, without warning, or after a long illness or physical decline. Whatever the circumstances, grief is not always lessened by the means of their passing.

Kath's husband, Les, had not been in good health for some time, but when he was admitted to hospital neither Kath nor Les believed that this would mark the end of his life. To Kath's disbelief, this was indeed to be Les's final hospital stay and, within days, he had died. Immediately after a death, the bereaved may feel as though they are caught up in a state of unreality and limbo, preoccupied with family and friends who rally around offering support, and the sheer volume of 'business arrangements' that demand attention. Shortly afterwards, however, life returns to normal for nearly everyone except for those still grieving, who can find picking up the pieces of their day-to-day lives extremely difficult. In Kath's case, the weather was no help. Deep grey winter skies added to her despair and Kath was left struggling to cope with jobs that still had to be undertaken.

One morning, standing in the bedroom, Kath was deep in thought, reflecting on the way her life had changed forever. Holding her husband's coat tightly, she gazed through the window at the deepening grey and mused upon the way in which it reflected her mood exactly. There were so many unanswered questions that tormented her. Was there hope of a brighter future for her? And just where was her husband at that moment – and was he close? As these thoughts flooded her mind, she was suddenly taken aback by the most extraordinary event. As she looked through the window, a flash of light burst out from the steel-grey clouds. It was unlike anything she had ever seen in her life and she still finds it hard to describe. 'It was,' she says, 'like deep yellow lightning.'

This huge flash of light filled the room and took Kath's breath away. It was the most wonderful sensation and allayed her fears instantly. Firstly, it was clear that this was no earthly light and could only have been a message from the angelic realms. Secondly, it convinced Kath that Les was near and taking care of her still through this sad time.

For many people this event would have been amazing, uplifting – a once-in-a-lifetime experience – but not for Kath!

Incredibly, the dazzling light appeared on many occasions and was not restricted to Kath alone. One day her brother, who had been wonderfully supportive and helpful, arrived to help her with some household jobs. As he was putting up some pictures for his sister, the same astonishing bright light flashed before his eyes as he was hammering into the wall. Initially he thought he might have hit a power cable, but admitted he had never seen a light quite like it before. Describing the experience to his sister, it was clear that this was identical to the light she had witnessed. Could it be that her husband was thanking her brother in this way for taking care of his wife?

On several other occasions, Kath has seen this brilliant yellow light, although now, a few years after her loss, it is becoming less frequent and less bright. She told me, 'It's as if Les is moving further away.'

He too has to move on and the angels must feel that by now Kath knows he is safely in heaven and they will always be close for her should she need reassurance.

~ AFFIRMATION ~

I will open myself up and allow the angels to bring light into my life.

∞∞∞

*There is a light that shines
beyond all things on Earth,*

*Beyond us all, beyond the heavens,
beyond the highest,*

The very highest heavens.

This is the light that shines in our heart.

CHANDOGYA UPANISHAD

Angelic Attunement

From the very earliest days of my research into angelic experiences, I have discovered that practitioners of reiki appear to have a greater proportion of angelically linked experiences than most. Reiki is an ancient Japanese art and a very powerful therapy; the Japanese word *reiki* relates to the universal life force. In reiki therapy, the practitioner's hands are usually placed on the recipient's body in a gentle and structured sequence in order to promote healing and emotional balance. The atmosphere of spiritual awareness generated by the practice of reiki appears to attract the angelic realms, perhaps providing a channel for contact with them.

One such dramatic event occurred when Linda was undergoing her final 'attunement'. An attunement takes place at the end of a practitioner's course in reiki. During it, the teacher, or Reiki Master, brings the day's learning to a close by performing certain essential rituals while standing behind the pupil. It is normal for this final session to be quite emotional and very spiritual in nature, and many feel a 'presence' or spiritual sensation, usually difficult to articulate.

Linda had been looking forward eagerly to the final day of her course and went along with high expectations. Little could she have known just how special it would be. As the day progressed Linda became aware of a lovely atmosphere in the room and that a sense of spiritual awareness pervaded it. Finally, the all-important 'attunement' began and, with her eyes closed, Linda was aware of the rituals that were being acted out behind her, centring above her head. When this procedure was complete, she opened her eyes. Nothing could have prepared her for what happened next. In her peripheral line of vision she clearly saw a huge span of white feathers – not small, fluffy white feathers, but enormous graded feathers, fanning out from floor to ceiling of the room. 'If this was part of an angel's wing, then it was a gigantic figure,' Linda says.

Instinctively, she sensed that this magical creature's wing was there to enfold her, totally enveloping her. Turning her head quickly, she expected to see some explanation but the vision had vanished within a second of it appearing. Interestingly enough, Linda was not at that point a firm believer in angels. Although she had kept an open mind on the subject, it was the very last thing she had expected to see at the end of that wonderful day. Her teacher, aware that something extraordinary had taken place, helped Linda to her feet. It was then that Linda discovered that her legs had turned to jelly. Feelings of elation, followed by a light-headed sensation, swept through her. It was clear to her teacher that Linda would require some help to become grounded once more. Very gently she was helped to come back down to earth.

'I can only describe what I felt as sheer elation,' Linda said. 'And this feeling stayed with me for a long time afterwards.'

It was a day Linda will never forget, for she had not only felt the spiritual love, but actually seen an angelic presence. It was a very special experience indeed and she can be sure that her own angelic visitor will be forever close.

An angel stood and met my gaze,

Through the low doorway of my tent,

The tent is struck, the vision stays;

I only know she came and went.

JAMES RUSSELL LOWELL

∽ AFFIRMATION ∾

*Today I accept that my angel is
ever close to my side.*

I arise today,

Through the strength of heaven,

Light of sun,

Radiance of moon,

Splendour of fire,

Speed of lightning,

Swiftness of wind,

Depth of sea,

Stability of earth,

Firmness of rock.

CELTIC AFFIRMATION

∞∞∞

Daniel and the Angel

Ever since the first humans evolved on earth, angels have been there, taking care of us. We only have to look at historical manuscripts and books from across the world religions to see that angels were prominent in the lives of the ancients. Indigenous peoples painted winged creatures or fashioned them from clay and wood. The Bible, in both the Old and New Testaments, records wonderful stories of angel appearances. There is, for example, the ultimate story of angelic rescue, which involves Daniel.

As a child attending Sunday school, I found the story of Daniel fascinating. Daniel was great friends with the king of the time, Darius, and many others were extremely jealous of him. A plot was hatched to fool Darius into passing a law that stated his subjects could worship only him. The penalty for disobeying the law was to be thrown into a lions' den. The devious group, aware that Daniel prayed to God, caught him in the act of worship and declared that he had broken the law. Sadly the king had to follow the law and Daniel was thrown into a lions' den, in front of which a large stone was rolled in order to ensure there was no way to escape. The following morning Darius rushed to the den and the stone was rolled away. To his delight, Daniel was found safe and sound. He explained that God had sent an angel who had closed the mouths of the lions and so he was saved.

> *She felt again that small quiver that*
> *occurred to her*
>
> *When events hinted at destiny*
> *being played out,*
>
> *Of unseen forces intervening.*

DOROTHY GILMAN

*Life is so generous a giver, but we, judging
our gifts by their covering, cast them away
as ugly, or heavy, or hard. Remove the
covering, and you will find beneath it
a living splendour, woven of love,
by wisdom with power.*

*Welcome it, grasp it, and you touch the
angel's hand that brings it to you.*

*Everything we call a trial, a sorrow, or a duty,
believe me, that angel's hand is there.*

FRA GIOVANNI

Angel Walkways

Since ancient times the labyrinth has held a fascination for mankind. Labyrinths appear in the art of many ancient civilisations, most notably the Egyptian and early Mediterranean civilisations. Labyrinths are also depicted in pre-Christian Celtic designs and Indian and Tibetan cultures. Today they can be found in many churches and cathedrals, such as the cathedral of Chartres in France, and are used increasingly in workshops as an exercise in weaving our way through the labyrinth of life. There is an almost magical feel to walking a labyrinth, which induces a state of concentration and meditation that can be very revealing.

A few years ago, I was with a group of friends in the Lake District on a beautiful warm summer's night. We laid out the pattern of a labyrinth using candles and, as the sky became dark and the stars emerged, they appeared to reflect the light of the labyrinth itself. Walking through this maze of light was a wonderful experience. It was, without doubt, a spiritual uplifting.

In such an environment, people can discover many things about themselves. Within a loving group, such as one sharing a workshop, inner feelings and memories have been revealed in a safe environment. Certainly this was the case for Sandra, who had initially only signed up to a workshop to support a friend.

Labyrinth of Light

Around twenty people were assembled to take part in a workshop designed to explore the role of the labyrinth in modern life. Although she was mainly there to accompany her friend, Sandra was intrigued; she knew very little about the symbol and was willing to learn more.

The labyrinth was laid out on the floor of the hall and eventually the time came for participants to walk the maze. Watching them, Sandra could not see exactly what the benefits of this might be and was rather surprised to notice one lady who had tears flowing down her cheeks. How very odd, she thought, and when her turn came she began this little journey with bemusement. Slowly walking along the lines, she found herself concentrating on her early life, her thoughts appearing to have risen completely out of the blue. The memories were so clear and sharp – painfully so – that Sandra was completely taken aback. Stopping in her tracks, she found moving forwards impossible, and was astonished to discover that she was rooted to the spot. It was at this moment that a light appeared to surround her, gently at first and then growing in intensity. The labyrinth had been encircled with candles and the day was bright and sunny. However, Sandra knew instantly that the light came from neither of these sources. Warmth engulfed her and she had the sensation that the painful memories, buried for so long, were melting away. A feeling of freedom filled her and she too found the tears rolling down her cheeks.

Discussing and sharing their experiences later, many people came to the conclusion that this simple practice of walking the labyrinth had induced the angels to step in and help. Many of them had experienced sensations of being lifted above everyday reality. Sandra found the sense of being freed from her past problems simply overwhelming. It was a very memorable day on which angelic light surprised one very grateful lady.

The Universe totally supports every thought
you choose to think and believe.

You have unlimited choices about what to
think. Choose balance, harmony and peace,
and express it in your life.

LOUISE HAY

Angel Feathers

I really think it would be impossible for me to write a book without including at least one or two white feather stories! Feathers appearing at significant times and in unexpected places are perhaps the most frequent of all angelic experiences, so much so that the white feather is often referred to as the 'angel's calling card'. Recently, I was invited to speak at the Festival of Mind, Body and Spirit. Ninety-three people filled the room and I asked how many of them had found a white feather and regarded it as significant. At least one-third of the audience raised their hands, proving the theory. Some sceptical people may laugh, saying, 'Had the cat brought the feather indoors or was there a passing bird?' – but it is not the source of these feathers that is the most significant aspect of the phenomenon (although many appear to be of a heavenly nature), it is when and where they appear. Timing is of the essence, as our next story illustrates only too well.

Angel symbols may be gentle or small
but never doubt their power and energy.

ADELE PERCIVAL

Sacred Feather?

On the face of it, perhaps a likely place for finding a feather might indeed be in church, falling from the rafters, but few people have ever reported seeing one while worshipping. For Paula, however, the feather that appeared in her church was of particular significance. Paula had found life confusing and difficult for some time, and now she was extremely worried about her daughter. There seemed to be no obvious solutions to the problems at hand and all Paula felt she could do about them was pray. This particular Sunday morning Paula prayed with an intensity and sincerity as never before, asking God and his angels to help. The service was rather long and involved, requiring the congregation to move around a great deal, standing and sitting, and approaching the altar rail to kneel down and receive communion.

Towards the end of the service there was a time for silent prayer and Paula asked once more for help with her dilemma. Opening her eyes, she was amazed to find a large, white feather lying in her lap! It positively gleamed up at Paula. A shiver ran up her spine as she realised that this was an instant answer to her prayers, that her angel had delivered her message without delay.

Thinking carefully about this experience, Paula mused that, the day previously, she had been into the church to arrange the flowers. The church was pristine, having been cleaned that day. She then considered the number of times she had moved around during the service – surely a feather would have fallen off her clothing had it been there earlier? Sitting next to her, her husband was also completely amazed, there being no rational explanation for the church feather. They both felt that it was a sacred feather in a sacred place, reinforcing in their minds the advice of the saying 'believe and receive'.

Be fully in tune with your spiritual essence,
sustained by a higher power.

Cherie Carter-Scott PhD

Venetian Feather

I would like to add a little feather story of my own. It's not a conventional one – that's for sure – but interesting, I feel. Recently I enjoyed a short break in the beautiful city of Venice. I set off with a group of friends, all of us in high spirits, looking forward to visiting this magical place.

Everything was going very well until our plane approached Venice airport and we realised just how dense the fog was. The pilot announced that the fog was probably too thick for landing but he was going to give it a try. Several nervous flyers in our party turned a delicate shade of white at this point; we were only too aware of the mountains all around. As the plane descended, the fog became thicker. Suddenly the pilot announced that landing was not going to be possible and our plane pulled up at startling speed, almost vertically – to the gasps of all the passengers. At this point the pilot announced, 'I may have to abandon this landing and we shall be forced to fly on to Trieste.' However, he continued cheerfully, he would circle round and give it one more attempt.

Only half jokingly, my friends turned to me and said, 'Glennyce, we need your angels – have a word, will you?' There were a good many more white knuckles clutching seats this time as once more we descended. The aircraft cabin fell totally silent as we plunged through the thick fog, Mercifully, this time we made it and, as the plane touched down, everyone burst into cheers and spontaneous clapping!

Giggling nervously, we left the plane and swiftly collected our luggage before setting off to the hotel. We were all in need of a strong coffee and, collapsing into the chairs in the hotel lounge, we ordered cappuccinos all round! The waiter brought two steaming cups to the table and we were amused to see that they had a heart design in chocolate on top of the froth. Four more arrived, all with a lovely chocolate heart on top, and my friends began to drink gratefully. This left just myself without a drink, but a moment later the waiter arrived with the remaining cup of coffee. Everyone gasped: instead of a chocolate heart in the froth, mine was covered with chocolate, leaving a white frothy feather on top! Amusing, but thought-provoking nevertheless; perhaps my angels were telling me they were taking care of us all the time!

There was a pause,

Just long enough,

For an angel to pass,

Flying slowly.

RONALD FIRBANK

* ✳ *

Light of Your Life

Coping with a serious life-threatening illness is difficult at any age but, if you have only just reached the age of sixteen, it is probably even more difficult than for most. Margaret recalls to this day, many years later, just how frightening the experience was.

Having been swiftly struck with considerable force by pneumonia, Margaret became dangerously ill. She says that describing this time is almost impossible for her, although she does recall the sensation of descending into a dark pit where no one could reach her. She was aware that her sister was close by, but she had the strange sensation of being close to her but unable to touch her.

It must have occurred to her family, and indeed to Margaret, that they were soon going to lose her as the illness steadily worsened. At this bleak point, the most amazing event happened, which Margaret recalls vividly even today. At the foot of her bed a bright light appeared, growing in intensity until it was the brightest light she could ever have imagined. In the centre of this light emerged a wonderful vision of an angel. The angel was incredibly beautiful, with a lovely smiling face and very long blonde hair that appeared almost to glow. So astonishing was the vision, however, that not only did Margaret see the angel but also the wonderful landscape surrounding her. There were huge ethereal trees, birds and other creatures, all bathed in an extraordinary light.

This experience proved to be the turning point in Margaret's illness and she gradually improved from that time on, until she was fully restored to health. She recounted the events to her parish priest, who told her this indicated the angel was telling her it simply was not her time to die. This was a perceptive and accurate summary of the wonderful experience.

Margaret has had many spiritual experiences throughout her life and visions that come in the guise of dreams have been particularly significant for her. One night she had a vivid dream in which her mother appeared to her. She urged Margaret to check for medical abnormalities in the form of a lump. Following these instructions Margaret did as she had been bidden and, to her astonishment, found a suspicious lump. Moving swiftly, she had this checked and, as she was undergoing treatment, the hospital told her that she was in fact very fortunate: if she had not discovered this abnormality at the time she did, it would have been too late to save her. So Margaret has been lucky to have had two visions with wonderful outcomes.

God committed the care of men and all things
under heaven to angels.

JUSTIN MARTYR

'Seeing' Angels

It may come as a surprise to some of us to learn that blindness won't prevent us from seeing angels. Research has revealed that many blind people have indeed seen angels through their internal vision, often referred to as the third eye.

Some years ago, I was privileged to share a platform with a world-renowned researcher in this field: D. Kenneth Ring. We were speaking at an angel festival in Philadelphia, USA, to a packed hall. Kenneth's work is fascinating and comprehensive, exploring the visions of countless blind people who have 'seen' angels. Interestingly, they tend to describe those angels in almost exactly the same terms as sighted people do – as also depicted in paintings, which of course they have never seen. This is a wonderful affirmation, confirming that angels are there for us all.

However, when researching this area, I also discovered that not only are the other four (or five) senses often sharper in the case of the visually impaired, but they have an increased tendency to recall angelic experiences that feature another sense, especially those of smell or hearing.

Our next story is unusual for two specific reasons. Firstly, the angel was seen vividly by the inner eye and, secondly, the angel was seen over a long period of time. Usually an angel is seen in fairly dramatic circumstances, and will appear only once. Occasionally, there may be a contact twice but even this is very rare. It is most unusual for an angel to stay with a person for any length of time and I have only encountered such an experience once before. This makes Heather's story very special and, I am sure you will agree, very inspiring.

Aspects of Angels

For a period of approximately seven years, Heather had been on a personal spiritual journey. She had found herself very involved in the practice of reiki, which proved to be a great blessing for her in many different respects. Never was this more true than when her husband became ill with cancer. The reiki treatments and care that she gave him proved to be extremely helpful, although sadly Heather's husband didn't regain his health. Slowly he became weaker. Nevertheless, he found that Heather's reiki treatments continued to give him peace and calm, which were very valuable at this stage of his illness.

On Boxing Day 2007 it was clear that her husband's situation was very serious, and Heather watched him slip in and out of consciousness. Giving almost continuous healing at this point, she concentrated on 'transitional healing' to help him onto the next stage of his journey. As she sat beside him, holding his hand, the most astounding thing happened. With her inner 'third eye', Heather saw the most incredible angel, unlike any she had seen in illustrations or heard anyone describe.

Instinctively, she recognised that the angel was female and extremely tall in stature. Very thin in appearance, she didn't have wings and was dressed in a dark blue gown. All around the angel's head was a wonderful, intense glow.

Heather knew this was a sign that her husband was about to die. This prompted her to explain to their children just how serious the situation was and they gathered with their mother around their father's bed. At 1.20 a.m. exactly, Heather's husband opened his eyes and, with an expression of laughter on his face, died. It was incredibly peaceful and a lovely end to his life, surrounded by his family.

Every time that Heather closed her eyes during the following days, there was the angel looking directly at her, with an expression of love and support. On the day of the funeral, Heather felt that the angelic presence was very close indeed and during the funeral she saw her angel each time she closed her eyes. Shortly after the day of the funeral, the angel appeared to Heather once more. This time, the figure was standing sideways, an unfamiliar posture as she had always looked directly at Heather. Heather felt this was a sign that she was about to leave; indeed, it was to be the last time Heather saw her.

The blue-robed angel had been the most wonderful uplifting presence, offering strength and support during a very sad time. Heather continues to offer healing, gaining comfort from the knowledge that she helps others whenever she is able. She also knows that, even though the angel is not visible to her any more, she is never far away.

꩜ AFFIRMATION ꩜

*Today, I concentrate on
my inner angel.*

꩜

Billy's Story

As we have seen, angels come in many guises – from enormous figures to a glimpse of feathers. Each encounter appears to be tailor-made for the individual situation and person – a sort of Bespoke Angel! Frequently these amazing encounters occur at times of life and death. They are designed to help us through life's most difficult moments.

Billy came into this world needing the angels with his very first breath. Luckily, his grandmother Joan was on hand to ask for angelic assistance urgently.

In the early hours of the morning of 28 September 1991, Joan's daughter was about to deliver her first baby. The doctor and nurses were in close attendance and Joan soon realised that this meant there was a problem. The baby was in distress and his heartbeats were giving cause for concern. Billy was delivered but it was soon obvious to everyone that the baby boy had died.

The hospital staff were clearly very distressed and Joan was at a loss to understand how this little one could lose his life before it had even begun. At this point, out of the corner of her eye, Joan spotted what she could only describe as a 'misty ball of light' suspended at ceiling height. Instinctively, she knew this was Billy's spirit in angel form and she silently implored that the little boy be given life. Gazing at Billy, she added, 'We will know how to look after you.' In that instant, Joan heard the baby give his first cry. After more treatment, he was handed to his mother to cradle in her arms, where he stayed all night.

A placid, lovely baby, Billy nevertheless had some problems when he was growing up. Each physical milestone came late in his development. The expression 'delayed development' gave his family hope, 'better late than never' being an encouraging thought. Although Billy has needed special people and special help along the way, the precise areas of help and the very people required have always appeared in his life, seemingly by coincidence.

Today, Billy is a college student and he enjoys many student activities such as hiking, rock-climbing and canoeing. He has a special gift: he can communicate with children who prove a challenge for most. Autistic children in particular respond to him. His sense of intuition is highly developed and he appears to perceive people's thoughts and needs with ease.

What a journey he has been on, from such a fragile beginning. Billy's confidence continues to grow as he is clearly being guided through life. Joan tells me that she firmly believes that it was the angels who gave Billy life that night when hope was fading fast. She believes they are close to him still, and few would disagree.

*Be not afraid but let your world be
lit by miracles.*

A Course in Miracles

Small Miracles

Here are some simple tips to help you see the wonders in your own life. Make a note of them in your Angel Book and consciously bring them to mind during the course of the next week or so.

* Today, remember the old adage that a journey of a thousand miles begins with the first step.

* Fly your own kite: the sky really is the limit.

* Age is only a number; it's the youthfulness of the heart that matters.

* Hold on to hope. You have no idea what will be around the next corner.

* 'To the extent we give to others, the universe answers in kind' (Judith Leventhal).

* Your angel is tapping you on the shoulder: stand still and listen.

* Make things happen in your life. There is no point in forever being a 'watcher'.

* Give yourself time each week to do what you love most. Each day is a special gift, which is why it's called the present!

* Start afresh from today. It is never too late to begin again: you have a whole, new, clean sheet tomorrow on which to write.

* Try to see the funny side. We all need a sense of humour.

If you have made mistakes, there is always another chance for you.

You may have a fresh start any moment you choose, for this thing called 'failure' is not the falling down, but the staying down.

Mary Pickford

* ✳ *

Train of Thought?

It is without doubt true that angels appear when we need them most. However, they do not always appear in a form we may recognise. It is only after the event that some people realise an angel was there to guide them. This was most certainly the case for Beccy, as her story illustrates.

It was a warm and rather sticky summer afternoon when Beccy climbed aboard her train. Leaving Manchester, she was aware that she would have to change trains at Sheffield in order to reach her final destination of Derby. As she settled into her seat, suddenly an image from her childhood rose to the front of her mind. It was so startlingly clear that it was as if she had pressed the 'replay' button in her thoughts. Catapulted back in time to the age of around six years old, she was dressed as an angel for the infant school nativity play. To her teacher's surprise, Beccy had requested that she should be allowed to sing. The teacher had offered to write her a line to speak, hoping this would appease her, but Beccy was adamant that she wanted to sing. Relenting eventually, the teacher had allowed

Beccy to perform 'Away in a Manger' and was dumbfounded to hear how beautiful her voice was; it was exceptional for one so young. That had been the start of Beccy's love of performing and she had gone on to take the lead in all the musical productions throughout her school years.

And here she was at the age of nineteen, travelling to take part in a festival of summer music that was going to include all types of musical styles and abilities. She sang all kinds of popular music and possessed a strong clear voice. However, although she had applied to several bands for the role of lead singer, so far she had been unsuccessful. If she had any regrets, it was that she longed to be part of a group. It would have been much more enjoyable to belong to a band of musicians and to be travelling with them, rather than alone, as she was now.

In the event, the outdoor concert in Derby was a huge success, helped by the lovely warm evening, and Beccy was well received by the audience. Feeling contented she climbed aboard the train for Sheffield where she was to change trains on her homeward journey. It was getting late when she arrived at Sheffield but she still had time to spare before the last train to Manchester that night.

Arriving on the platform she was a little surprised and concerned to find that she was the only person there. It was lonely and dark. It was, however, late and she told herself it would not be unusual for the station to be fairly deserted. At that moment an announcement came over the loudspeaker, saying, 'The last train to Manchester has been cancelled and any passengers should make their way to the front entrance of the station, where a bus will take them to Manchester.'

In near panic, Beccy ran to the station entrance. It was a

large station and she had to cross several bridges over the tracks to get there. Arriving at last at the exit, she watched with dismay as the bus disappeared into the distance! There was not a soul about; despite her knocking on a couple of doors and shouting as loudly as possible, no one appeared and Beccy had not the faintest idea what to do next. Tears rolled down her face as she stood rooted to the spot with fear.

Suddenly, she became aware of a gentle hand on her arm and, turning, she saw a tiny old lady standing before her. 'It's all right, dear,' the lady said. 'Come along with me.' And, with a firm grip that belied her stature, she propelled Beccy back to the platform from whence she had come. The platform was as bleak and deserted as before and, finally finding her voice, Beccy told the old lady that the last train for Manchester had gone. 'No, dear,' came the reply. 'There will be another.'

Astonishingly, once more there was an announcement, this time saying that an extra, single-coach train would be arriving shortly at their platform and that it would be a non-stopping train to Manchester Piccadilly! As if by magic, the tiny single-carriage train appeared and Beccy leaped aboard with the old lady. The train was clearly preparing to leave immediately. At the very last second a huge commotion on the platform heralded the arrival of six young men, who hurled themselves into the carriage in breathless confusion. Sitting several seats in front of Beccy, the old lady turned to smile at her encouragingly. That moment the train departed and Beccy relaxed.

The young men quickly struck up a conversation with Beccy and she was interested to learn that they were all part of a group. They had been performing in Sheffield that evening and after the gig had discovered to their dismay that the old van they used would not start. Abandoning it, they had dashed to the station in the hope that there would be a late train back to Manchester. Beccy was delighted to hear about their music and she explained that she was a singer travelling home from a festival. Before the train reached Manchester, the pleasant young men had invited Beccy to contact them, with a view to her auditioning as their lead singer. The amazing coincidence of meeting these young musicians on her way home was mind-blowing for Beccy. The evening, which had taken such a frightening turn, appeared to be ending on a very optimistic note.

Arriving at Manchester, Beccy remembered the old lady as she stood up to leave the carriage. She had been so caught up in the conversation that she had completely forgotten about her. Turning to say goodnight, she was astonished to see that the single carriage was completely empty, save for herself and the six young musicians. That's impossible, she thought. The train hasn't stopped since Sheffield.

Perhaps the old lady was in the train loo? But no, that was empty – as the open door testified. It seemed like a complete mystery, but by now Beccy was so tired that she fell into a taxi for the short journey back home and waved goodbye to the young men, promising to ring the following day.

Sleeping soundly until fairly late the following morning, Beccy woke to find her flatmate had already left for work. She wondered if she would be interested in her adventure. Making a cup of coffee, Beccy once more thought about the old lady, and several startling facts occurred to her. Firstly, where on earth had she come from? She had no luggage and was not even carrying a handbag! Secondly, how did she know Beccy had missed the train to Manchester? Beccy certainly had not told her. Finally and most mysteriously, where on earth had she vanished to? There was simply no logical explanation for her to disappear the way she had done. It was all very odd.

Ringing a member of the band, however, she was thrilled to be invited to audition as promised, but before ending the conversation she asked the young man whether he had seen where the old lady on the train had gone. 'What old lady?' was the reply.

'The one sitting near me on the train when you fell through the doors,' she laughed.

'There was no one else in that little carriage but you,' came the reply, 'certainly no little old lady. Had you been drinking?' he jokingly asked.

Beccy felt a shiver run down her spine: she knew at once what had happened. She had met her very own angel, who had guided her home and arranged for her to meet the musicians with spiritual synchronicity. She had come a long way from that six-year-old singing like an angel to meeting her very own angel.

Yet 'I have been guided from that very moment,' Beccy decided and said 'Thank you' out loud for all the love and guidance.

I will give thanks for my angel,
no matter where or how
she may appear.

An Angel's View

You may want to light a candle before settling down in your favourite chair for this meditation. If you have a scented candle, so much the better.

Relax and breathe deeply, letting your cares and worries float away with each breath you exhale. Picture yourself sinking into the chair and becoming as one with this comfortable, familiar piece of furniture.

Visualise a tranquil beach scene: a long, flat white stretch of sand and the deepest of turquoise seas lapping against the shore. The air is full of the scent of the sea, fresh and clear in your senses. Walk slowly along the beach until you arrive at a rocky promontory. Gently step around this headland and you will see waiting for you on the other side a gloriously coloured hot-air balloon. The balloon is striped with the seven colours of the rainbow and suspended beneath it is a strong wicker basket.

Step into the basket and relax as the balloon begins to ascend into the blue sky. You feel secure, unafraid and protected as you soar ever higher. Looking down, you see the most beautiful scene: the white sand and sparkling sea, patchwork fields and trees now appearing toy-like with altitude. You realise at once just how beautiful the earth is and how fortunate you are to live there.

Soft music fills the air and you sense instinctively that this is an angelic chorus. Looking up, beyond the balloon you see angels reaching as far as the eye can see into the blue sky, and you know they are there to support you. A thousand angels glowing white, gently singing, linking you to another world.

Slowly your balloon begins to descend and the angels fade from sight. You land on the white shore with a gentle bump and, climbing from the basket, you feel refreshed and blessed. Glancing up at the now clear sky you are only too aware that, although you cannot see the host of angels, they are neverthe-less always there, watching over you.

Walk slowly on the sand, retracing your steps around the rocky outcrop to find yourself once more alone on the beach where you started.

Sink back into your chair and become aware of the room and slight sounds outside. Slowly open your eyes and stretch before blowing out your candle. Your spirits feel as light and buoyant as the rainbow-striped balloon. Hold on to that feeling and float through your day.

Sometimes I go about in pity for myself,

And all the while,

A great wind is bearing me across the sky.

Ojibwa chant

Inner Vision

Do you recall a time in your life when you felt especially happy? Is there a particular occasion you can picture vividly in your mind? It might be a day when you were very small, playing on the beach, building sandcastles and hunting in rock pools with a shrimp net. Or you might prefer to remember a day in your teens when perhaps you passed an important exam that would open future doors for you. How about when you passed your driving test or fell in love for the first time? You might think of your wedding day, a special landmark birthday, a journey overseas or a wonderful Christmas celebrated with loved ones… Whichever happy day you choose, picture it clearly in your mind. What were you wearing? What was the weather like? Who was with you on that special occasion?

See in your mind's eye the happiness on your face and remember how that felt inside – the wonderful joy welling up inside you.

Hold on to that feeling. You experienced such happiness once and there is no reason why it cannot happen again. Happiness comes from within so choose to be happy; choose to be positive as you recapture that wonderful day once more. Believe that happiness can and will be yours again. Should you ever doubt this, recall again the vision you have in your mind now.

*The greatest part of our happiness or misery
depends on our dispositions and not our
circumstances.*

MARTHA WASHINGTON

* * *

The Gift of Sight

As the stories in this chapter make clear, there are many
different ways of 'seeing'. Even people with twenty-twenty
vision may be blind to the signs and symbols placed in their
lives by the angels. To correct imperfect 'angelic vision', we may
simply need to train ourselves to notice the spiritual love all
around us in our daily lives. We may spot signs in nature, from
rainbows to animals, birds and feathers, which can strike us as
significant and can all be evidence of angelic intervention.
Sometimes we will be contacted by our inner angel and see him
or her with our mind's eye.

As we have seen, an angel's appearance may range from a
glorious, huge figure surrounded by light, to a less dramatic
shape without wings. According to the evidence of those who
have seen them, angels can be dressed in many different
colours and hues. Pure white light of an unearthly brightness
may be witnessed by some. Others may see intense yellows,
blues or lilac accompanying an angelic form. Finally, there are
those angels who appear in everyday dress, looking exactly like
everyone else – just as Beccy discovered when she was helped
by the old lady.

These 'ordinary' heavenly messengers often step in when we are in need of help, usually in busy and confusing situations. Then, we may find that we are helped swiftly and seconds later our rescuer has simply vanished. When reporting these events, people often describe the angel as having 'piercing blue eyes' or an air of unusual calm about them.

Not to be forgotten are the angelic qualities that we may find in our loved ones, friends and colleagues – all have an inner angel and we may just have to look carefully before we see it.

Sight is a precious gift and, however we may use it, always give thanks for the sheer wonder it brings.

The golden moments in the stream of life
rush past us, and we see nothing but sand;
The angels come to visit us and we only know
when they are gone.

GEORGE ELIOT

Personal Insight

There are many everyday expressions that mention sight, but that do not mean seeing literally. To realise the full implications of a situation is referred to as 'seeing the light'. A loved one may be described as 'the light of one's life'. When we are confused, we may not be able to 'see the wood for the trees'. Many of these expressions allude to inner sight, and the truth is that it's essential to take a good look inside ourselves – our hearts and our minds – at certain points in our lives.

Assessing a situation and addressing issues that need attention, instead of hoping they will simply 'go away', can be fruitful and exhilarating. If we are working too hard, heading for 'burnout', taking a good look at our situation may prevent disaster. Often we feel driven to continue on our treadmills, becoming more and more stressed, yet unable to stop the vicious cycle. That is when it's time to stop and think, appreciate our gifts and talents and then use them for our own and others' pleasure, letting our light shine through.

When life becomes difficult, share your worries with a close friend or family member – and rope them into a little adventure as you explore new paths towards happiness. We each of us only have the present, so do not put off taking steps to achieve your dreams. Even those modest ambitions you have been pushing to the back of your mind deserve attention: get them out and dust them off, then go for it!

* ✳ *

And the trouble is,

if you do not risk anything

you risk even more.

ERICA JONG

Thank You for Sight

Why not create a 'Sacred Space' in your home to remind you how fortunate you are to be able to see the gifts that have been given to you in life?

First, choose a space that can be exclusively yours – perhaps a window sill or mantelpiece in a bedroom, conservatory or spare room. Place special objects in this space. You might, for instance, include a cherished photograph of those you love, a favourite book, a brightly coloured candle, ribbons, a small ornament you love, or an intriguing piece of driftwood. Add whichever items move you, which strike you as beautiful and which are somehow close to your heart. Arrange them in a manner you find pleasing and, if possible, take a few moments each day simply to look at them and reflect on the special gifts and magic the world has to offer.

Although they may not always be visible to the human eye, the angels are there for us, whenever we look for them.

CHAPTER 2

The Sound of Angels

*Angel voices ever singing round thy
throne of light.*

*Angel harps forever ringing
rest not day or night.*

FRANCIS POTT

There are myriad ways of hearing angelic messages. A voice is, of course, the most obvious form and many people have heard angelic voices offering comfort and guidance. The voice can be external – a physical noise – or be heard in a person's mind; whatever its form, it is usually so clear that the person hearing it is left in no doubt that it relays a message from an angel.

A voice from heaven may be far from gentle and sweet. Angels often use loud, insistent tones in order to make people take notice of them immediately. This is for the immediate protection of those concerned, such as individuals caught in dangerous situations that require dramatic action. However, gentle voices may also be heard when the occasion demands. A soft reassuring voice can be heard by people trapped in difficult circumstances.

Similarly, sounds in nature frequently relate to angelic presences. I once attended a meditation evening where we were played whale song. The experience was haunting and moving. It made me very aware of just how important sound is in the natural world and how it can reach out to us spiritually.

Birdsong in particular has touched many hearts. A certain type of bird may hold a special significance for somebody: it may then appear to that person and sing at appropriate moments, usually when comfort is needed. Pope Gregory I is famously reported one morning to have heard birdsong so beautiful he felt it could only have been sent by God. Inspired by this experience, he wrote the Gregorian chants.

Sitting by a gurgling stream, or walking through a wood and hearing the rustle of leaves as the wind blows through the trees, can likewise be awe-inspiring moments. The sound of the sea is also very moving and evocative. If you are fortunate enough to live close to the sea you will know at first hand how wonderfully soothing the sound of a wave-lapped shore can be. Most of us will recall wonderful days and evenings on holiday, perhaps lying in bed, listening to the sea through an open window.

Naturally, music is another medium that automatically comes to mind when speaking of angelic sounds. In paintings, angels are frequently depicted playing harps or trumpets and it is easy to imagine them playing wonderful music in heaven. Friends of mine in California have a large artwork hanging in their hall that I find particularly fascinating. Rather than showing a traditional angel with a harp, it is of a figure bending over a flower, as if listening to it. The whole scene is pale grey and blurry. I remarked on how mysterious I found this painting and yet how moved I was by it. My friends told me that the artist was deaf. Then it all fell into place: the blurry landscape, the figure bending his ear to the flowers. It seemed to me that the artist was trying to depict his world and it made me very grateful for the clarity of mine.

Music and angels are so closely linked that angelic encounters often contain heavenly sounds as well as sight. When describing angelic experiences, many people recall hearing amazingly beautiful music – with no apparent source. This can be sweet and low, barely audible, or it may fill the room with swelling sounds of spine-tingling sweetness. The sound of tinkling bells is frequently reported, as is the harmony of uplifting angelic voices, unlike any usually heard on earth.

However, as incredible as these otherworldly sounds may be, we should not dismiss music from very earthly sources, which may also carry angel messages for us. This may take the form of a song heard on the radio or television. It may be a particular piece of music, poignant and personal – for instance, a special song shared with a loved one who has passed away – but the inspiring aspect will always be the timing of when it is heard. In the form of an angelic message, it will be heard at a significant moment when we need to be uplifted or comforted. It could be music from a specific time in our lives when we were especially happy and now we yearn for those times again; hearing it reminds us of them and offers us comfort. The miraculous timing is spiritual synchronicity and if we pay attention to this phenomenon we will notice it with increasing frequency in our lives. Concentrating on the experience and meditating on it afterwards will enhance the experience. (You may wish to follow a guided meditation below, which focuses on the sounds of angels.)

History rings out with the sound of songs and compositions dedicated to angels. Harp music is especially evocative of heavenly beings; however, even pop music contains many references to angels. You would amazed by how many pop songs contain the word 'angel'. Perhaps the most well known is Robbie Williams' hit 'Angels'. There doesn't appear to be a wedding today at which his song will not be played as some point in the proceedings.

It seems that the angels will occasionally join in earthly music themselves: a story in this chapter describes an angel taking part in a song. And I have even heard stories in which entire choruses of angels join in with the singing of human choirs – with awe-inspiring results. There are also examples of musicians visiting loved ones after death and relating how special and amazing they find the music in the next world. It would certainly seem that the sounds of the angels are all around; we only have to tune in and listen carefully.

The Universe is always singing,

And man must learn to listen,

So that his heart many join the
universal chorus.

SARAH MARTHA BAKER

Home

Diane was driving to one of her favourite places in the whole world – the English Lake District. For more years than she could remember, Diane and her family had visited this lovely area each spring and it had never failed to renew their spirits. The place was so special that, when her husband Colin had died, Diane and the family had decided to scatter his ashes on top of the fells where he loved to walk.

Music had played a large part in Diane's life and she had sung in choirs for most of her adult life. The family as a whole, however, had an eclectic taste in music and one of their favourite artists was Mick Hucknall, of Simply Red. Mick Hucknall's song 'Home' had been played at Colin's funeral service and, as Diane thought about it now, it seemed an appropriate choice.

As she approached the cottage that held so many special memories for her, the fell where Colin's ashes had been scattered came into view. Suddenly the familiar sound of Mick Hucknall singing 'Home' came over the radio airwaves. There was no mistaking the message – it was a moment of perfect spiritual synchronicity.

Angels need not wings
For they soar on the current of love
everlastingly.

ANON

A Meditation on Angel Music

Choose a moment when you know you will be alone in the house. Light your candle and sit comfortably with your hands resting loosely in your lap. Either concentrate on the candle flame or close your eyes, calming your breathing as you do so.

You feel the air warm and soft against your skin and, rising before you, you visualise a long flight of stairs that you are invited to climb. This presents no difficulty at all because you feel strong arms supporting you as you climb. Reaching the top, a dark sky surrounds you, velvet blue and quite beautiful. You feel safe and warm, enveloped in this wonderful darkness. The blue light is pierced by thousands of tiny twinkling stars, gently floating towards you and swirling around you in a whirlpool of light.

From a distance there comes the sound of music, gentle and sweet, and it increases in volume as it approaches you, until it too surrounds you. The starlight and the music are now intertwined and encircle you like protective wings. You know your angel is with you.

Do you recognise the music? Does it hold a special significance for you? As the vision of circling starlight fades, keep the music in your heart as a gift from the angels. In your mind, slowly turn around and retrace your steps down the flight of steps until you are once again sitting in your own chair. Take several deep breaths, stretch your limbs and blow out your candle. Be happy in the knowledge that you can return to this special place of light and sound whenever you wish.

Take time to be friendly –
it is the road of happiness.

Take time to dream –
it is hitching your wagon to a star.

Take time to look around –
it is too short a day to be selfish.

Take time to laugh –
it is the music of the soul.

OLD ENGLISH PRAYER

Heavenly Harmony

The meditation above brings the expression 'the music of the spheres' to mind. The ancient Greek philosopher Pythagoras believed that, taken together, the movements of the planets created a heavenly harmony. Whether they do create their own music or not, the planets and the stars are important angelic symbols. We tell people who shine in life that they are 'stars' and we 'look to the heavens' for encouragement in our own lives. On the other hand, when our spirits are low, we speak of 'feeling down'. Here is a story that describes the power of the stars in raising our spirits.

The Man Who Sold the Stars

In the spring of 2008 I was invited to be a guest speaker at the international Festival of Angels in Munich. The venue was a beautiful converted monastery, where I enjoyed two days filled with other speakers, musicians and artists. It was an interesting occasion: each presenter had a different approach to the angels, as well as to the ways in which the angels can help us to find inspiration in our lives.

One evening the audience was treated to a presentation from a wonderful Israeli storyteller, who captivated everyone with his lovely tales. The stories were enchanting, but they had a strong moral element, which made me really think about them. I was so captivated by a story called 'The Man Who Sold the Stars' that I would like to share a brief version of it with you now.

The story is set in a small Russian village which was very poor and very cold. An all-pervading air of melancholy hung over the village and the villagers walked with their heads bowed, staring at the ground. No one smiled, for life had given these people precious little to smile about.

One day a stranger arrived in the village and set up a simple stall in the central square. On the stall were many brightly coloured paper stars. The notice in the centre of the stall read 'Stars for Sale'. The people looked perplexed until the man explained that they could buy the stars for a pittance. Moreover, each paper star represented one visible at night in the heavens. The people loved the idea.

When they stepped forwards to make their purchases, the seller would point to the sky and explain that they had bought such-and-such a star. Soon all the people in the village had bought a paper star and had turned their faces up to the sky, searching for their star's counterpart. Their faces were shining and for the first time in many years they were happy, as they looked up towards the heavens.

We can all learn from that star seller and look up: if we change our perspective, things are rarely as depressing as they first appear. 'Look to the stars' is great wisdom indeed.

A cluster of white stars, silvered against
the background of the blue velvet sky
force their way into my eyes and into
my heart.

MARC CHAGALL

* * *

~ AFFIRMATION ~

I open my ears to the
sound of angels.

How to Hear the Angels

It can be difficult to hear what the angels have to say to us when we are distracted by the soundtracks of our busy lives and the chatter of our own thoughts. Here are some easy ways to bring their music into your life.

✳ Drive alone into the countryside or walk in a local park. Listen to the sounds of nature.

✳ Think of a piece of music that holds a special significance for you. If you are able, play the music; if not, let it run through your head. Choose this as your angel music and make a note of the next time you hear it played.

✳ Promise yourself a trip to a concert featuring your favourite type of music.

✳ Promise yourself you will listen out for your own 'inner voice', through which your angel can communicate with you.

✳ Pay close attention to birdsong and see how many birds you can identify by their song.

✳ Know for certain that the angels love you, and their messages are there for you – just believe.

Laura's Story

At the beginning of this chapter, I talked about nature's sounds and how significant they can be if we listen carefully to them. Well, this was particularly true for Clarice, the grandmother of Laura.

Laura was a very beautiful little girl who brought joy to all. When this lovely little girl died at the tender age of eight, the devastation her family felt can only be guessed at. However, Clarice had shared some golden moments with her granddaughter and the memories of these helped her cope with her grief. She shared the following story with me when we met at one of my workshops.

It had been an annual treat for Clarice, her husband and Laura to visit the Blackpool illuminations. Children are especially enthralled by this magical display of lights, and Laura was no exception. Their weekends together in Blackpool became the source of many cherished memories.

Five years passed after losing Laura before Clarice and her husband felt they had the strength and courage to return to Blackpool. They hoped that an autumn weekend break there might even play a part in the healing process. That Sunday evening after dinner, Clarice decided to walk alone to the sea front to watch the sun go down. The sky was suffused in a beautiful orange light as Clarice listened to the water lapping gently onto the shore. A feeling of peace and contentment filled her as she pondered the fact that they had spent the weekend at Laura's favourite place – and coped. At that precise moment, Clarice heard her little granddaughter giggle, the sound coming from over her right shoulder.

It was exactly the same giggle that would fill the air when Laura had been taken for fun rides on the pier. Then, her grandparents would shout encouragement to her as they watched her whirl round on the ride and her delightful giggle would fill the air. The happiness Clarice felt at that moment was overwhelming – her own little angel contacting her in their very special place.

Clarice told me she is very happy to share this wonderful experience not just with me but with all the readers of this book in the hope that they may find inspiration and comfort from this amazing event.

Stress Busters!

Angelic encounters often involve hearing an inner voice. Listening to an inner voice is something that we can all experience, but we rarely find the time to stop and listen to it. And when we do we are often too ready to dismiss its message as being only the product of our imagination. However, learning to trust our own inner voice can lead us to greater awareness and angelic insight.

Take some valuable time out of your busy schedule and connect with your own inner voice, look at the following list and contemplate including one of these items into your routine...

* Take a long, hot bath with soothing music playing and lots of fragrant oils to help you relax.

* Go to the cinema to see a film that will give you the 'feel-good factor'.

* Invite a friend round for coffee or meet in a local

coffee bar for an hour just to catch up and chat.

✳ Listen to a favourite piece of music alone, in a quiet corner of the house, maybe with a glass of your favourite drink to help you unwind.

✳ Think of something you have always wanted to do … and do it!

✳ Go out for a meal – even if only to a simple, affordable café – with someone you love.

✳ ✳ ✳

What is this life if, full of care

We have no time to stand and stare?

WILLIAM HENRY DAVIES

Angelic Satellite Navigation

I have literally lost count of the number of times that people have told me they've heard a voice directing them while driving. It seems that, if they take notice of it, the voice always leads them away from danger.

Trevor's story is very typical in that respect. As a busy businessman, he often spent his days rushing around the country for meetings and conferences. On this particular day he had been in his office since early morning, working on a business presentation, and as the late afternoon approached he was still trying to get it ready. He would be delivering it that evening at a conference in a venue over a hundred miles away. He knew he was cutting it fine when he finally set out and was well aware that even if the traffic was in his favour he would arrive only just in time.

Mercifully, the motorway appeared to be free from heavy traffic and the stream of vehicles moved smoothly along. Trevor gave in to temptation and put his foot down. He found himself with a virtually clear stretch of road ahead of him and flew along in the fast lane. Suddenly, he heard a voice from within the car telling him to move into the slow lane. It was loud, clear and insistent. Shaking his head in disbelief, certain of course that he was alone in the car, he ignored the voice.

For a second time the voice warned him – even more loudly than before – to move away from the fast lane at once. Shaken, Trevor did as he was bidden, slowed down and moved across the lanes. At that very moment, a large lorry travelling from the opposite direction inexplicably lost control and broke through the central reservation barrier. It careered across the lanes, passing immediately behind Trevor, before coming to a stop.

All the traffic, including Trevor, came to a halt and soon a police car appeared on the scene. Thankfully, owing to the light amount of traffic on the motorway at that time, no one had been hurt. The lorry driver himself suffered no ill effects. Even the policeman declared this to be a miracle.

Trevor shook with shock at the realisation that, had he not obeyed the voice, the lorry would have broken across the barrier and without a doubt hit him head on! He could only conclude that he had heard an angelic voice and he offered a silent 'thank you' for its help.

Over eight years have passed since the incident and Trevor tells me that it marks the only time that he has heard an angelic voice. However, he also says that now he is more aware than ever that he is being looked after.

~ AFFIRMATION ~

I will listen to my inner voice
whatever my circumstances.

❦❦❦

A Voice of Reason

Although rare, angelic voices may be heard for many different reasons. Interestingly enough, there are some lucky people who hear angel voices on several occasions in their lives.

One day, while she was preparing Sunday lunch in her kitchen, Gaye heard a voice with a very moving message. The voice simply said, 'Dad's home.' Without thinking, Gaye said aloud, 'No, it's far too early.' Walking from her kitchen, she went to a window that looked out onto the drive at the front of the house, where she saw her husband parking his car. It was then she realised with a start that the voice had belonged to her daughter Heather, who had died several years previously.

On another occasion Gaye was sitting quietly in her armchair, reading, when a voice said to her, 'Send it to Jackie.'

This only made partial sense; although Jackie is Gaye's sister, she had no idea what she was supposed to send to her!

Pausing in her reading, she thought about the message, then dismissed it and carried on with her book. Once more the voice spoke to her, louder and more insistent. This time Gaye acknowledged it, asking, 'What must I give to my sister?'

To her astonishment the voice told her that she should go upstairs, where she would find what her sister needed at the present time. All at once Gaye understood what the voice meant. She made it a practice to keep a certain amount of cash in her bedroom for emergency purposes and she knew that this money must be sent to her sister.

Acting at once, Gaye sent the money to Jackie. The following morning Gaye received a phone call from her surprised sister, asking how on earth she knew that the cash was exactly what she needed. Due to unexpected circumstances her sister was struggling financially and Gaye's gift was most welcome.

This story is a good illustration of the expression 'God send'; in this case, the messenger was God's angel, telling Gaye of her sister's need.

Angels are messengers and ministers.

Their function is to execute the plan of divine providence, even in earthly things.

SAINT THOMAS AQUINAS

Musical Note

Earlier in this chapter, I shared Diane's touching story about hearing a song that reminded her of her husband. As it happens, hearing music at particularly appropriate moments is a fairly common angelic experience. If it should happen to you, please don't dismiss it as 'mere coincidence'!

Caravan

France held a strong fascination for Julie and David. Every summer they would hitch up their caravan and drive to their favourite country, where they would stay as long as possible. After retirement, they were able to holiday in France for many weeks each summer. It was exciting to pack up and leave home, knowing there were no deadlines to meet in terms of their return.

On the journey music was very important to them and they would take along all their favourite CDs to play. One of their favourites was 'Caravan Song' sung by Barbara Dickson. They would play it when they first set out on holiday and when they began to make their way home: it appeared to suit the mood and the occasions perfectly.

To reach home, they would drive through the magnificent grounds of Castle Howard, famous for its role in the TV series *Brideshead Revisited*. At the top of the stately home's long hill drive, the vista before them was of the entire Ryedale valley, where they would always stop to take in the view, happy to be nearly home.

Sadly, one spring a few years ago, David suddenly died. Julie was stunned. Some time after the funeral, she decided to take stock of her situation. As their home was in an isolated, if beautiful, part of the UK, Julie decided it would make sense to move house to be nearer her family. Having lived for twenty years among the wonderful scenery of the Yorkshire Dales, she knew it would be a wrench to leave. However, the arrangements were eventually made and Julie moved to South Yorkshire. Leaving friends and a much-loved cottage was never going to be easy but it still felt like the most sensible thing to do.

A little time passed and Julie gradually settled down in her new home, where she counted her blessings for her family and good new friends. One day she was invited to travel back to her much loved village to meet up with some old friends and she set out with very mixed feelings.

Driving once more through the grounds of Castle Howard, she came to the top of the long hill and stopped, as she and David always had done, to take in the view. To her astonishment, at that very moment the familiar voice of Barbara Dickson singing 'Caravan Song' came over the radio. It was a spine-tingling moment. Julie couldn't ever recall hearing that particular song on the radio before – or indeed since. It was clearly a special case of spiritual synchronicity.

Immerse Yourself in Heavenly Music

Sit in a comfortable chair in a warm room where you can feel calm and undisturbed. Take several deep breaths and concentrate on the air entering and leaving your lungs. Starting with your feet, curl your toes tight for a moment and then relax them until you feel almost as though they are sinking into the floor. Then tighten your calf, thigh and stomach muscles, releasing them in turn. Move on through your hands, arms, neck and shoulders until your whole body is relaxing into your chair.

See yourself in your mind's eye: you are standing on top of a hill in the far north and, although it is bitingly cold, you cannot feel it. Wrapped warmly in furs and basking with an inner glow, you look ahead, your eyes scanning the sight before you. The sky is navy blue and cloudless. Across the heavens dance the colours of the Aurora Borealis, the Northern Lights. They are luminous greens and blues, and are constantly changing in shape and size.

Most remarkably, these lights appear to be broadcasting a heavenly music which sounds like the song of the angels. Lit up by these magical lights, the trees and hills glow and sparkle in this landscape of snow and ice. You realise just how beautiful nature is and how the beauty is all for you.

Keep the music and the light in your mind's eye as you are gently transported through the snow and twinkling light. The angel song surrounds you as you feel yourself returning to your own home and your comfortable chair.

Slowly open your eyes and allow your breathing to return to normal. Stretch and enjoy the sensation of being totally refreshed.

There is evidence to suggest that people who live in the areas where the Aurora Borealis can be witnessed on a regular basis not only see them but often hear music coming from them too. In the far northern Alaskan town of Yellow Knife a high proportion of the population report this to be the case – and believe that they have heard songs from the angels.

What know we of the blest above,

But that they sing, and that they love?

WILLIAM WORDSWORTH

You Only Have to Ask

Nearly everyone agreed that Verity had a lovely, sweet voice – the only trouble being that Verity herself chose not to believe it. Confidence eluded her, although there was no obvious reason why this should be the case. A pretty and intelligent little girl, Verity was popular with her peers and well liked by her teachers. Her parents and especially her grandmother tried valiantly to assure her she was talented and much loved.

Mrs Taylor taught Verity music and eventually persuaded the little girl to sing in the end-of-term school service in the local village church. Verity immediately regretted agreeing to perform; however, her grandmother knew that if she managed to summon up the courage, just this once, then it would boost her confidence enormously in the long term. And so it was decided that Verity would go to her grandmother's house as often as possible to practise the little song she was to sing. The service was a whole month away, which would give Verity plenty of time to become note perfect.

The day of the service arrived and poor Verity felt so nervous that her parents and grandmother feared she might just back out altogether. Soothing words and a great deal of encouragement got them all to the church. As she watched her granddaughter take her place, getting ready to sing for the congregation, her grandmother's heart went out to her. She closed her eyes for a second and asked the angels to be with her little Verity. The organist began to play and Verity began to sing in her clear, sweet voice. After the first few notes, she visibly relaxed and her grandmother smiled with relief. It was at this point that another voice joined in from just behind where her grandmother sat, softly and sweetly singing the same song. Turning around sharply in surprise, Verity's grandmother was amazed to find only an empty pew behind her. Yet the voice was unmistakably there in her ear.

Verity had by now reached the final chorus and was singing with great confidence. The mysterious voice carried on singing and finished at exactly the same time as Verity. Looking up, her grandmother saw the beaming child walk back to her seat among approving nods from her teachers. It was only then that it dawned on her that the angels she had fervently asked to help had indeed been in the church with them. Not only had they calmed Verity and helped her to sing like an angel, but they had even joined in for the benefit of Grandma!

It is the song of angels sung by earth spirits.

E. W. H. MEYERSTEIN

How to Hear Your Angel

What are the sounds that have made you extremely happy? Do you have a favourite pop star that maybe you once went to see in concert? Can you remember listening to an orchestra playing a wonderful piece of music and can you recall how that felt? Did the sound send a shiver of happiness down your spine?

A friend recently told me that the most wonderful thing she has heard in a long time was her little grandson saying, 'Grandma'; it filled her with such happiness. Perhaps this was also the case for you – or maybe it was hearing the voice of a loved one for the first time in a long time. Maybe a close friend said something so sweet and kind you felt an inner glow.

Do the sounds of nature fill you with awe and joy? Are you moved by birdsong or the sounds of waterfalls and streams?

Recall an event in which sound made an important impression on you. Focus on how, through the medium of sound, you felt immense joy. Hold on to that thought and those feelings – and realise that life can be filled with such moments if we choose. The happiness you felt on that occasion can be yours again. Life is wonderful and is there for living. Just take a moment to be still and hear the angels.

'Stay' is a charming word in a friend's vocabulary.

LOUISA MAY ALCOTT

Listen to Yourself

Do you really listen to yourself? Do you listen properly to your body, for instance? Do you ever feel strains and stresses, but choose to ignore them? Do you ever ignore that inner voice telling you to slow down or, conversely, to speed up? Do you need to take more exercise – stretch yourself physically while helping yourself mentally?

We read all the time about the power of endorphins, which create the 'feel-good factor' when we exercise. And it's common knowledge that a brisk walk always makes us feel better, not just because of the physical exercise, but also because of the lift it gives to our spirits. (Incidentally, for any dieters out there, physical exercise not only increases your metabolic rate but continues to raise it for many hours – and even days – after the exercise has been taken.) Common sense also tells us that carrying on with a daily routine instead of resting an injury will make the injury worse, resulting in a longer period of healing. Yet many of us do just that – we carry on in spite of backache and headaches etc., being stoical about our injuries, when we know inside that our body is saying, 'Stop!'

Is your inner self nagging you to take action about an ongoing problem? Do you tell yourself, 'I must get the ache/pain/problem seen to', while having no real intention of acting upon the thought? Listen, now is the time: your body is precious and the only one you have! Pay attention to your inner self, take good care of yourself and make sure you have enough rest and sleep. Listen to yourself and take your own advice; then give your angel a chance to speak through your inner voice too!

The quieter you become
the more you can hear.

BABA RAM DASS

* ✳ *

Give Thanks for the Gift of Hearing

Make time once in a while to treat yourself to a moment in which you can immerse yourself in a wonderful sound. You may wish to play a CD of your favourite piece of music or turn on the radio. Or perhaps you have a bell you could ring? Or do you even own one of those wonderful Tibetan bowls that you can make 'sing'? Perhaps you own a drum; beating a drum makes for a dramatic and a powerful way to appreciate sound and hearing.

If you prefer something gentler, an early springtime morning may reward you with the wonderful sound of birdsong. Walking in the country will make you only too aware of nature's myriad sounds: cows mooing, the bleating of lambs or the fast-flowing water of a stream or waterfall.

Enjoy the sound of children playing, even the roar of a plane overhead, and literally thank God for your ears.

CHAPTER 3

Fragrant Angels

*P*erhaps the most gentle of all angelic interventions takes the form of fragrance. This can be so subtle that at times it leaves people wondering if they have imagined it. Others, however, find an angelic fragrance to be so distinctive that there can be no doubt about its origins. I have heard such fragrances described as unique combinations of flowers, spices or essential oils that are, quite frankly, beyond description.

A particular scent may be associated with the loss of a loved one, such as the perfume a much missed person wore, or the fragrance of a flower or spice connected with somebody who has passed over. It may be possible to detect these smells at curiously appropriate moments, even though the person with whom they are linked is no longer there. Similarly, tobacco smells may waft around a room even when no one present is smoking, or there may be the aroma of cooking when the kitchen in not in use. If a person is grieving, these wonderful aromas will often occur on the loved one's birthday or the anniversary of their death.

Hospitals have documented particular fragrances that are sometimes detected when a person has just passed away; these fragrances are often reminiscent of lavender or violets.

Interestingly enough, violets have long been associated with medicine and healing establishments. The violet was the ancient symbol of Athens and the Greeks used it extensively in the treatments of headaches and sleeplessness. Medieval priests cultivated violets in their monastery gardens and used them to relieve swelling or hoarseness. The blue violet is said to represent love. Perhaps all of these associations are linked to the scent detected at hospital bedsides. In any event, a fragrance such as this may bring comfort in times of worry or anxiety, and if we believe that it is literally heaven-sent, then it is a lovely reassurance that we are not alone.

Fragrances and spirituality are inextricably mixed. The nativity story explains how the Magi brought the gift of frankincense for the newborn baby Jesus. In temples and churches around the world, incense perfumes the air. Some indigenous peoples also include aromas in sacred rituals. When we light joss sticks and candles in our homes today, we mimic those rituals in some respects; if scented, the candles bring an additional sense of comfort, as well as light and warmth. As Jim PathFinder Ewing says, in his book *Finding Sanctuary in Nature*, a book of wisdom about Native American traditions:

> In modern Christian churches, the lighting of candles, the waving of the incense and the singing, are done not only because the candles are pretty, the scent sweet or the songs beautiful, but also to bring the worshippers' intent to a point at which it can draw the beings present fully into the moment ready to experience the eternal now, where power resides.

Fragrances have a power of their own. When we smell them, they can stir up our memories and transport us to other places and people in the blink of an eye. Holiday happiness may be captured by a certain smell, such as the sea, or the scent of exotic flowers not grown at home.

Throughout the year, important occasions are associated with particular fragrances. Imagine Christmas without the smell of pine trees or all the wonderful aromatic foods associated with the festival. Weddings wouldn't seem the same without the fragrance of flowers filling the ceremony space. Halloween simply would not be the same festival without its rich assortment of smells – of pumpkins, treacle toffee, sweets and fruits.

Fragrances are inextricably linked to our memories and moods. In their wisdom, angels know how to use fragrance as a valuable tool with which they can communicate with us.

Angels are like flowers in the forest, beautiful,
fragrant and found only if we seek.

ANON

Fragrant Protection

Many practitioners of aromatherapy and reiki have angel stories to share. It seems that the fragrances they use and the spiritual atmosphere created in their treatments somehow invite the angels to be present. Laura's story, which follows, is about one such experience.

One beautiful spring morning, Laura was preparing her reiki treatment room for her first client of the day. Recently she had purchased some perfume sprays, which she planned to use before starting the reiki healing.

The first client was a close friend called Rosemary, who was feeling rather fragile as she had recently lost her job and was struggling financially. That morning, she wanted to unwind for a short time and forget her worries. Laura looked at her perfumed sprays and chose one especially for her friend. The bottle had the name of an angel written on the label, which Laura thought would be especially appropriate. Gently spraying the air above Rosemary, she told her to close her eyes and relax.

A moment later Laura held her hands above her friend's head, concentrating on transferring the wonderful energy she could feel in her hands. She became aware of the room brightening, which she thought odd owing to the fact that sunshine was already streaming through the window. However, the light continued to increase until it was so bright that Laura could only marvel it did not hurt her eyes at all.

Suddenly, the dazzling light formed itself into a pair of huge wings, hovering above the treatment bed. Yet her friend seemed completely unaware of what was happening. It was true that Rosemary had her eyes shut, but Laura thought the light would have penetrated even closed eyelids. There was no movement from her friend, however, and Laura could only gaze in wonder at the fantastic sight. The fragrance increased with the light, making the moment even more magical.

Slowly the vision faded and Laura continued with the treatment, saying nothing to her friend until she had completed the session. As her friend slowly sat up on the treatment table, she said to Laura, 'There was such a strong sensation of love in this room, I feel blessed.' Only then did Laura tell her what she had witnessed and Rosemary left her that day feeling calm and comforted, knowing that she had the help and love of the angels with her.

Silently one by one, in the infinite
meadows of heaven

Blossomed the lovely stars,
the forget-me-nots of angels.

HENRY WADSWORTH LONGFELLOW

Breathe in the Scent of Angels

Choose a fragrant candle and position it safely in a room where you will be undisturbed. If you have fresh flowers in the house, place them alongside the candle.

Light your candle and sit comfortably for a few moments, enjoying the sight and fragrance of the candle and flowers. Take several deep breaths and close your eyes.

You see yourself walking slowly along a path leading to a small wood. It is springtime and the birds are singing in the trees above. As you follow the path, the trees become denser, but the light is dappled and bright, and you feel completely at ease. Reaching a clearing, you notice an old, large stone wall directly ahead, in the middle of which is a large wooden door in the shape of an arch. Push the door open and walk through. On the other side you discover a beautiful stone building, completely round in shape, and as you walk towards it you see the shape of the door is also arched. Push the heavy wooden door open and walk into the circular building.

A wonderful sight greets you: in this beautiful round room there are many stained-glass windows and the sunshine streams through them, casting exquisite patterns on the stone floor. The whole room resembles a kaleidoscope. Take in this lovely scene, marvelling at the beauty.

As you adjust to the colour in the room you become aware of a small round table in the middle of it. The table is covered with a deep red, velvet cloth and on it is a wooden casket, the size of a jewel box. You walk over to it; clearly you are meant to open the lovely box, so you slowly reach forwards and lift the lid. As you do so, instantly the air is filled with the most wonderful fragrance, swirling up and around, completely encircling you.

Peeping inside you see that the box is filled with flower petals but unlike any you have ever seen or smelled before. There is the sensation of a presence in the room and you feel certain this is an angel.

Thank the angel for the beautiful experience, place a handful of the petals in your pocket and take a last look at the sun-dappled colours in the circular room.

Leave the room, closing the door behind you, and slowly walk to the stone wall. Pass through the wooden door and then take the path through the wood. You feel peaceful, happy and totally safe.

Once more become slowly aware of the room and the chair in which you are sitting. Breathe deeply and slowly open your eyes. Blow out the candle and keep the image and sensation of the fragrant angel in your mind.

How shall we tell an angel
from another guest?

How, from the common worldly herd,
one of the blest?

Hint of suppressed halo, rustle
of hidden wings

Wafture of heavenly frankincense,
which of these things?

GERTRUDE HALL

Aromatic Angels

Here are some simple ways to help you become more aware of the fragrances in your daily life and of the ways in which the angels can reach you through them.

* Meditate with a fragrant candle and ask the angels to be present. Notice what sensations come up…

* Bake a loaf of bread, enjoy the aroma and ponder on life's essentials.

* Take a long, lingering walk in the park, taking in all the wonderful fragrances and the scents of the trees, shrubs and flowers.

* Relish the smell of coffee percolating and ask a friend to join you for a cup.

* Treat yourself to some beautifully perfumed toiletries and take a long, luxuriating scented bath.

* Buy a lavender plant and place it by your front door in spring – the fragrance as you leave home each day will be uplifting and lingering.

* Arrange evergreen branches and pine cones in your home – the wonderful smell is not just for Christmas.

* Simply give thanks for your wonderful sense of smell.

*I am aware of nature's gift of
fragrance at all times.*

∼∽∽∽

The Scent of Life

A complete loss of smell appears to be less common than impaired sight, but can nevertheless be very distressing for the person affected. Smell and taste are inextricably mixed so a person without a sense of smell may be unable to enjoy certain foods to the same degree that other people can.

A friend of mine recently had to undergo hospital treatment and found that his medicines removed his sense of smell. Having never seriously thought about this particular form of sensory deprivation, he could not believe how difficult this made his life. He couldn't smell the wonderful aroma of cooking, his garden flowers or his wife's perfume, and even his sense of taste was altered. He also realised that the loss might lead to personal danger, as he would be unable to smell leaking gas, for instance, or dangerous chemicals. He found that his world had taken on a new and worrying aspect. Angels would, I feel sure, contact people who suffer in this way through their other senses, especially those of sight and touch.

Discover the blessings you already have.

CHERIE CARTER-SCOTT PhD

Discover Fragrant Happiness

You may already suspect what I would like you to do at this point! Your task now is simply to recall fragrances and smells that evoke pleasant and happy memories for you. For instance, spring lilacs may stir your memories of childhood, or scents from the garden may bring back memories of another happy time in your life. Perhaps the smell of the sea transports you to holiday heaven? Were you a 'Bisto kid' – does the smell of certain foods bring back the vision of happy family meals? Does the smell of pipe tobacco remind you of a much-loved grand-father? Do some scents remind you of particular people? Can you remember the perfume your mother used to wear?

Close your eyes for a moment and let the memory of a fragrance fill your nostrils. Allow the warmth of the memory to envelop you and recall the happiness that the smell evoked. Place yourself at the very heart of those wonderful memories and experience again the wonderful feelings of happiness associated with them.

When it comes to the experiences of your senses, keep an open mind: they may be a clue to the ways in which your angel is trying to reach you. You were happy then, you can be happy again – hold tight to the fragrance. It might just be the fragrance of your angel.

The soul should always stand ajar,

Ready to welcome the ecstatic experience.

EMILY DICKINSON

*Happiness is a perfume you cannot pour
on others, without getting a few drops
on yourself.*

RALPH WALDO EMERSON

* ❋ *

Scented Candles

In recent years, I have been very interested to witness our growing fascination with candles. They are extremely popular gifts and many homes now have several placed around the house. I cannot help but think that these lovely objects, with their connotations of church and worship, are reminders of more spiritual times. In the past candles were routinely lit during mourning to represent the deceased's soul ascending to heaven, and many people believed that, when the commemorative candle was blown out, an angel would be in the smoke to guide the departed soul to the afterlife.

However busy our everyday lives today, it seems that most of us look for a connection with something profound when tragedy strikes. After a tragic accident, for instance, wayside shrines spring up immediately with flowers and candles. These improvised shrines seem to offer much comfort to grieving relatives and friends.

I read recently in the *Observer* newspaper an article by the well-known journalist and broadcaster Kathryn Flett. She wrote movingly about attending the funeral of her friend James, who had died suddenly at only forty-nine years of age. Mingled with immense sadness, the service also reflected the joy and privilege of all his friends at having known this young man. Through her tears, Kathryn felt the urge to light a fragrant candle for James and the all-pervading fragrance filled her home for weeks. The symbolism of the flame and the wonderful aroma both brought comfort to her. I am certain that Kathryn will always feel close to James and that the happy memories will soon come flooding back whenever she lights that particular candle.

I know of healing groups who will, at the start of their session, light scented candles for people they feel need healing in one form or another. Meditation groups will usually focus on a lit candle, the light and particularly the fragrance helping their concentration. Similarly, many alternative shops and festival stalls sell little phials of liquid said to represent one or other of the angels. The spraying of these produce a lovely aroma and atmosphere for a meditation group or individual.

Angel Scent

Make yourself comfortable in your favourite chair. Relax your body, starting with your feet: contract your muscles tightly and then relax them as you exhale. Follow this by contracting your calf muscles, abdomen, arms, neck and head muscles. Feel your body sinking into the chair.

Recall one memory that is linked to a special, significant fragrance. It could be anything – a church service, a holiday or a party. Simply concentrate on the fragrance connected to the memory. Embrace the sensations of comfort and familiarity, and let the happiness of that time wash over you. Close your eyes and visualise a tall, glowing angel surrounded by bright light and a wonderful aroma. Is it the same fragrance as the one you recall from the past? Does this vision remind you of times that were less complicated and more pleasurable? Promise yourself during this visualisation that you will allow yourself more time to enjoy the wonderful fragrances all around you.

Open your eyes and give yourself time to think about how this might be achieved. Are there some botanical gardens within reach of home where you might spend a day? Perhaps you could visit a local garden centre and buy a plant with particularly sweet fragrance to fill the house. A walk in a bluebell wood in spring would be a magical experience or even a trip to your local market might be rewarding. If the market sells an array of beautiful flowers, treat yourself to a bunch. There are plenty of roses out there – you only have to stop and smell them!

As the moths around a taper,

As the bees around a rose,

As the gnats around a vapour,

So the spirits group and close,

Round about a holy childhood,

As if drinking its repose.

ELIZABETH BARRETT BROWNING

* * *

Growing Angels

I have always thought that the most enjoyable form of transport
is the train. A sense of freedom accompanies train travel as it's
possible to a walk about, visit the buffet car, stretch the legs and
meet other people. When catching a train I usually feel a sense
of adventure, as if going on holiday; the whole experience
whisks me back to childhood.

I have also met some very interesting people when I have
travelled on trains, and heard some lovely angel stories. One
morning, when I was travelling down to London, our train
pulled into a station. An announcement informed us that, owing
to engineering works, we would have to disembark and then
catch the following train in ten minutes' time. With accompanying moans and groans, we all alighted.

A young man stood next to me on the platform and began
to chat. He was worried that he was going to be late for a
meeting he was due to attend. However, the promised train duly
arrived and we climbed on board, where I found myself sitting
next to the anxious young man. As he calmed down, he realised
that he would reach London only fifteen minutes later than
planned, allowing him lots of time to arrive at his destination.

During the course of our journey, our conversation turned
to gardening. The young man told me that his adored grandfather had taken him with him each week to his allotment,
where he taught him about growing all manner of things.
'Whenever I see an allotment, I think of my grandfather,' he
confessed.

To my surprise, he then asked me if I believed in the afterlife
– in spirits and angels! Smiling, I assured him that a great deal

of my life was associated with that very subject and that I had written many books about it.

He explained that he had been only twelve years old when his grandfather had died and that he still missed him desperately. The funeral had been a great ordeal, he added, as his young mind had tried to grasp where his grandfather had gone – if, indeed, he had gone anywhere at all!

He told me that one Saturday morning, several weeks after the funeral, he had been feeling extremely sad. In the past, Saturdays would have been spent with his granddad at the allotment and now instead he found himself alone in his bedroom, close to tears. To his surprise, the most amazing aroma suddenly filled the room. It was a mixture of vegetables, herbs and flowers; in short, it summed up the warm and familiar smell of the allotment. So powerful was this aroma that it seemed to envelop him. Then, in an instant, it was gone.

He was totally astonished by the event, but never doubted that it meant that his grandfather was connecting with him in a way he would understand. He asked if I thought people could become angels and if his grandfather was now an angelic being, able to contact him. I was happy to tell him about the many examples I have uncovered during my years of research and that I do indeed believe that our loved ones go on to become guardian angels.

At this point, we pulled into Euston station and everyone hurried to leave the train. Smiling his thank you, the young man shot away with the parting remark: 'Put that in a book if you like!' I didn't have his name or contact number to talk to him about it again, but I am including his story in this book in the certain knowledge that his grandfather will be watching over him to this day.

Every moment in our day,

Every breath we take,

Every fragrance we sense

Is infused with the angels.

NICOLE ERRINGTON

In Praise of Fragrance

In chapter one, we discussed how to make a sacred space in your home in order to appreciate fully the gift of sight. This time I recommend creating a sacred space through which you can remind yourself how wonderful it is to be able to smell. Fill it with fragrant items, particularly those that conjure up special memories for you.

You may wish to refresh the space every now and then by replacing the items in it. In spring, for instance, you could make the focus of your space a fragrant candle or you could use one of those lovely sprays that are attributed to a particular angel. In the summer, you could place a vase of sweet-smelling flowers there or a seashell that retains the aroma of the ocean. In the autumn, you could arrange items collected during a woodland walk.

Allowing your thoughts to rest for a few moments in this space once a week will remind you of how very fortunate you are to have the gift of smell.

~ AFFIRMATION ~

I will always accept
fragrant messages.

∞

Everyday Aroma

You may have heard of people – usually women, it is true – being referred to as 'fragrant'. This instantly conjures up an image of someone lovely in both appearance and manner. Is it possible, I wonder, to describe someone's life as 'fragrant'? Are there people who lead charmed lives in which all aspects are lovely? I think it unlikely, although some people do appear to be blessed with fewer worries than the rest of us. However, the truth is that we all face challenges in life. This is when we should ask ourselves if we might have missed a message sent to help us in the form of a gentle fragrance.

I have a feeling that, rather like humans, angelic beings eventually cease to try to contact us if they are continuously ignored. Sadly, a subtle angel sign that has been tailor-made for us may not be repeated if missed the first couple of times round. On the other hand, if we accept the sign for what it is and acknowledge the fact that it is sent by an angel or a loved one who has passed over, then there is every chance that it will be repeated for us.

If this has been the case for you – if a mysterious scent has appeared at a time when you most needed a sign – then there is something you can do about it to acknowledge its impact. It is usually very helpful to try a simple meditation, ideally using a fragrant candle, in which you ask the angels to repeat the message. Believe that the sign was meant for you and then believe the angels will answer your call for their help.

May you have a fragrant life!

CHAPTER 4

A Taste of Heaven

*A*t first, it may seem as though the sense of taste has little to do with spirituality. On the face of it, taste would probably be the last of our faculties that we would associate with the angels. However, in that case we would be wrong: taste, especially in connection with food and drink, is closely linked with the spiritual aspects of our lives. Food and drink are associated with rituals in virtually every world religion. Moreover, my research has taught me that many people experience a strange taste in their mouths when aware of an angelic presence.

Taste is also linked to our personal journeys through life and to specific rites of passage. On hearing that a baby has been born, one of first things most families will do is toast the new life – preferably with champagne! – and give thanks. Baptism in one form or another often follows, where a celebratory cake is eaten after the ceremony. Should we be Christians, when we are young we may celebrate a First Communion with communion wafers and a sip of wine, which represent the body of Christ. We will often celebrate our birthdays and other special occasions by sharing a special cake with our loved ones.

The Jewish tradition sees boys taking part in Bar Mitzvah

ceremonies and girls in Bat Mitzvah, with special foods as part of the proceedings. On Friday evenings when leaving the synagogue, it is believed that an angel will accompany the worshippers home for the Friday family meal, should they have been sincere and devout during their prayers. If the individual can maintain the level of devotion and concentration achieved in the synagogue outside it, then the angel will protect them all the coming week.

Weddings follow a similar pattern as other rituals, with wine and cake being the principal ingredients of the wedding feast. At Jewish weddings, sugared almonds also feature strongly. The custom of throwing these sweet nuts to guests spread to most of Europe through the arrival of Sephardic Jews from the Iberian Peninsular. Today, at many Jewish weddings, regular sweets are thrown as a reminder of those sugared almonds.

Finally, whatever our faith, when we depart this world our family and friends may join together in a meal after the funeral service.

As the seasons unfold, certain foods and drink mark spiritual occasions throughout the year. Pancake Day dates back to the time when people would use up their supplies of eggs, milk and flour before beginning of forty days of abstinence during Lent. Easter itself has many symbolic foods that are linked to the Resurrection and also to pagan beliefs, which nevertheless had spiritual significance. Easter eggs are the symbols of new life and chocolate rabbits are linked to fertility.

The significance of harvest festivals is self-explanatory, not only for the offering of food but for the harvest suppers themselves which are enjoyed throughout the land. The festival of Diwali with its spicy delights follows them in the year and

Hanukkah also offers edible delights. All these events are linked to celebratory foods and wouldn't be the same without them.

In many households, a grace is said at the beginning of a meal in order to ask for a blessing on the food and for spiritual as well as bodily sustenance. In some societies today, monks hold out bowls in which to receive offerings of food, trusting to divine help and the goodwill of others to provide for them.

Offering food and drink is a strong tradition in many societies. Countries all around the world have their own particular foodstuffs for welcoming guests, through which people demonstrate affection as well as giving sustenance. Perhaps unsurprisingly, throughout history many people who have performed good deeds and been of service to their fellow men have been linked to food. Take the chocolate industry, for instance. As well as being a member of the famous Fry's Chocolate Company, Elizabeth Fry was a prison reformer. Similarly, the Cadbury and Rowntree families were Quakers and 'social justice' employers. The fair trade movement today spreads goodwill and fairness through the spirit of free trade – it literally embodies good taste. Early soup kitchens were established by spiritually inspired people and offered a service that is still needed today. These socially minded pioneers were willing to pass sustenance to the needy because of their beliefs.

If people want to get in touch
with their angels, they should help the poor.

LAWRENCE CUNNINGHAM

Food for the Soul

The Bible is peppered (if you will pardon the pun!) with numerous references to food and drink. There are miracles such as Jesus turning water into wine and the feeding of the five thousand from five loaves of bread and two fish, to name just the most well known. In the Old Testament, the Israelites were fed 'manna from heaven' when they were trudging through the wilderness. Manna is actually a delicious, sugary derivative from the tamarisk bush. The substance crystallises from the bush early each morning, falling to the ground. The timing, however, was the significant thing in the Bible story, for it was when the Israelites most needed food that they found this amazing bush and unsurprisingly attributed their discovery to divine intervention.

Food is frequently an analogy for spiritual sustenance. We talk about 'soul food', 'bread of heaven', 'drinking at the font of spiritual knowledge' – the imagery and associations of food are deeply ingrained in our everyday thinking. If we add to this all those foods that have a spiritual reference in their names we shall see how strongly the link is forged: there is angel cake, angel cookies, angel hair pasta, to name just a few! We often describe our favourite foods as 'heavenly' or as tasting 'divine', like the 'food of the gods'.

Food and drink are also associated with healing, with nature offering many examples of plants and herbs that heal. Modern medicine owes a great deal to nature, often taking basic plant material and turning it into effective medication. Certain herbal drinks are known to be calming and can help in many ways, from treating insomnia to helping heal rashes on the body.

Today, food is seen as a preventative for many modern diseases. We are advised to eat five portions of fruit and vegetables each day to keep us healthy and disease at bay. It is not a fallacy to say that the state of mind of the person cooking alters the taste and the quality of the food. Preparing food in a peaceful frame of mind makes a meal taste sublime. Anyone who has made a meal under duress, in a hurry, or for people not particularly liked, will know that it will frequently turn out a disaster.

Most importantly, however, food is an expression of love. This doesn't just apply to eating out as a gesture of romantic love on Valentine's Day, but to love between families – and particularly love between a mother and child. Nurturing is often expressed by cooking and baking for children, and the happiness it gives mothers to see their children eating and thriving is well known. Jewish and Mediterranean people are perhaps particularly aware of how they are encouraged to eat traditional food at the family table and play on this in their many 'mother and food' jokes. All mothers, of course, will relate to this and feel relieved and happy to see their children grow healthily in response to their nurturing through food and its links with love.

Many cooks and chefs have told me that the act of cooking is itself enhanced by adding love to the recipe. One thing is certain – food, love and angels make for a heavenly mix. Where there is love in any situation, the angels are never far behind.

Recipe for Love

Cookery programmes are very popular today and it seems there is no end to the amazing concoctions that modern chefs can whip up. One thing is for certain: in spite of all the glamour associated with it, cooking can be very tiring work.

Certainly, when Brian decided to attend catering college he had no idea just how much hard grind would be involved in his course. However, despite the long hours spent learning his craft, Brian discovered that he really loved cooking for others. Blessed with a kind and giving personality, he had been brought up in a household where food was lovingly served by a mother who took great delight in seeing her family enjoy a home-cooked meal. The meals were, he says, a means of sharing family love.

When Brian got his first job in a respected restaurant he experienced nerves and excitement in equal measure. The first day was daunting and, though he felt proud and very grown-up in his official 'whites', underneath it all he was terrified. Dedicated and determined to make a success of this job, which he felt sure would lead to a good career, he adjusted quickly to the long days and frantic pace in the kitchen. Weeks flew by and soon he felt competent and trusted as his employer gave him more and more important tasks to do. Happy and contented, he pressed on and worked very hard indeed.

One day, the head chef told Brian that a very important party of eight would be arriving at the restaurant for dinner that evening, adding that everything had to be perfect. Brian set about making the desserts with excitement. However, when he discovered that the meal was for a celebrity who was treating his family to a birthday meal, Brian's excitement was threatened by an extreme attack of nerves. Nevertheless, he was determined to put all his energy and every effort into making this a special meal and, as he admired the celebrity, he decided that he would put a lot of love into the mix as well.

The evening drew on and the desserts were about to be served. Having put all his skill and love into their making, Brian found himself feeling peaceful and fortunate to have such a rewarding task. Finally, as he lifted his creation onto a large, heavy plate – hands shaking – he was suddenly taken aback by a very odd sensation. It was as if another pair of hands was helping him to lift the plate. This was impossible, of course, but the sensation lifted his spirits immensely.

Brian told me this story and asked if I thought this was an angelic or spiritual experience. I told him about a chef in London I had met several years earlier, who tried to put as much love into his cooking as possible and who felt tingling in his hands when he did so. He believed this to be the response of the angels, adding their love to the process.

A huge smile lit up Brian's face and he said, 'That was exactly what I thought might be happening, but I was afraid to say so in case people thought I was mad!' He explained that the evening had been a huge success and the special guests had complimented the staff on the excellent food, singling out the dessert for extra praise.

Now, not only has Brian chosen the right career for himself, but he knows that he has help from a magical source – especially when including his unique ingredient!

The Food of Angels

Find a moment one morning before leaving the house or before the chores of the day encroach. Sit comfortably in your favourite chair in a room where you will not be disturbed. Light your scented candle and focus on the flame, or close your eyes and enjoy the fragrance. Take several deep breaths and relax into the chair. See with your mind's eye.

It is early morning and you are walking alone by the side of a river in an old, quaint town. The entire population is still sleeping as you slowly make your way along the riverbank. The river is lined by trees and the morning sun's rays shine through the leaves, making dappled patterns on the ground.

You arrive at a large stone building, clearly very old. To your surprise, you notice the large wooden door is open. Instantly you are aware that this is an invitation for you to step inside. You find yourself at the beginning of a long corridor and as you slowly walk along you are suddenly conscious of a wonderful smell, warm and comforting. Eventually you reach the end of the corridor in this silent building and you push open a large door. You step inside and find yourself in a huge, warm kitchen.

The room is completely empty and as you slowly make your way around you realise that the wonderful smell is emanating from a covered dish placed on the central wooden kitchen table. Peeping under the cover, you see a beautiful little cake, golden brown and covered with flakes of chocolate. Clearly it is meant for you so you take the cake and raise it to your mouth.

Biting into it is the most wonderful sensation – light and rich at the same time – and you feel a tingling sensation on your tongue. You have a sense of a presence as the surrounding smell turns from one of food to something that is at first unidentifiable. You know it is linked to your angel and that the food is a gift to satisfy your hunger and fill your soul.

Turn and leave the kitchen, eating your wonderful cake. Return down the long corridor and out into the sunshine of the riverbank. The air is still and the town has not yet awoken. Walk slowly, enjoying the sunshine and the peacefulness, eating your wonderful cake. At last you arrive home and slowly come back into the room.

Blow out the candle and be aware of the angel's gift: you have experienced a little taste of heaven.

Holy Food Orders

I was fascinated to read a headline in the newspapers recently which said that 'TV Nuns Cook by the Good Book'! It was an account of two Spanish nuns who had risen to celebrity status by cooking on Spanish television. In a show called *Taste of Heaven*, they revealed the secrets of their wonderful cooking. The programme was filmed in the Spartan convent kitchen, using very ancient utensils and even more ancient recipes. The article said that, unlike the slick productions of most modern TV shows, these simply presented programmes reveal the level of devotion and love put into all the nuns' preparations.

Monks, of course, have been famous for centuries for brewing wonderful beers and other forms of alcoholic drinks. Even the very name Benedictine demonstrates this. Although these drinks are made to help the monastery survive and provide remuneration, the love devoted to the operation is never in doubt. For many people food, drink and love are inextricably mixed.

*I will not miss the opportunity
to act like an angel by bringing
bounty into people's lives.*

֍֎֍

*Eating nutritious food supports you in living
lightly and energetically within the body.*

*In taking care of the body, you take better care
of the spirit.*

MARIANNE WILLIAMSON

Taste the Joy of Giving

There are many different ways in which we can celebrate the gift of taste in our lives. By becoming more aware of the role that taste plays in our lives and the pleasure it brings, we will also become more sensitive to the many ways in which the angels can connect with us through this important sense.

* ✳ Bake a cake and give it to a loved one.

* ✳ Bake a cake and give it to someone you don't
  know, such as the staff at the local charity
  shop maybe, as a thank you for the work they
  are doing.

✱ Teach a child how to bake cookies. Enjoy the messy process!

✱ If you think it will please them, buy a sandwich or a hot coffee for a *Big Issue* seller or charity collector.

✱ Donate a box of fruit to your local Salvation Army hostel.

✱ Take a box of cakes or cookies to work for colleagues.

✱ Give a bag of sweets to a policeman or traffic warden – make them feel loved for once!

✱ Tactfully offer to cook a meal for someone struggling financially, physically or emotionally.

✱ Donate some homemade soup to a soup kitchen in the city.

✱ Invite all your family or friends round for supper, feed them and tell them how much you love them.

*When we perform a charitable deed or
benevolent action it doesn't disappear into a
vacuum or a spiritual black hole – ultimately
we can expect it to be repaid. Sometimes we
are repaid within a matter of moments or
hours after executing the kindness and can
immediately see the connection between our
deed and our reward.*

JUDITH LEVENTHAL

Cup of Love

Food often reminds us of a certain place in our lives. A wonderful holiday in a foreign country can be instantly recalled at home if we eat the sort of food we enjoyed while we were there. Similarly, particular types of food can be linked to special times and people.

I often used to hear my extended family talk about the food they ate during the war years and how, even though the time marked the height of austerity, they relished the ingenuity required to make a tasty meal. So much so that sometimes they actually pined for those ration-driven meals.

Thinking of links between people and food, I recall an offer that was promoted by a famous soup company some years ago. If you bought several packets of their instant soup and saved the labels you could send the labels to the head office along with a small fee, for which you received a ceramic mug. This mug had the slogan 'hug in a mug' on it and the handle represented a pair of hugging arms. I sent one to a much-loved friend I had not seen for some time, just as a joke to make her smile. However, on the day I posted the mug I received an identical one from the same friend. It was so lovely to receive a hug through the post! Using the mug often, I would sip the soup and feel the love.

As well as reminding us of our present friends, the aroma of certain foods can promote sheer nostalgia for childhood – although I had better steer away from school meals! For one young lady, eating food that reminded her of childhood and her loved ones led to a remarkable experience.

A Taste of Home

Whether it is because of the rolling mists that shroud the fields each autumn or the dry summers, New England produces the most delicious blueberries. According to Connie, they are simply the best in the world. She grew up eating these wonderful berries in many different recipes and, even as an adult, happy memories of her grandmother would flood her mind whenever she saw the rich-coloured fruits. Hot blueberry pie with ice cream or blueberry muffins were Connie's favourite and Grandma often had both waiting for her when she used to visit as a little girl. Now, however, it all felt so very long ago.

Connie's Grandma had died and her family had moved across the Atlantic to live in London, where her father had a new job. Here she was, many years later, preparing for what was to be a big day in her life. She had packed her suitcase in preparation for her journey north to Leeds University, where she was going to begin a degree course. Once more she would be starting out in a new place, having to make new friends in a strange city.

However, Connie was excited about her course and realised this was a great opportunity to strike out on her own. Her parents helped load up the car and off they went on the first stage of Connie's big adventure. When the time came for her parents to leave her in the halls of residence, saying goodbye proved to be more difficult for them than for Connie herself. As she looked round her new room and met her fellow students, she felt her spirits rise and excitement take over from her nerves. A feeling of being in the right place settled her and she knew instinctively that she would be happy in her new life.

Time passed and Connie found that she was very happy, the usual ups and downs of student life notwithstanding. She coped very well and towards the end of the first term she found herself in a relationship with a young man. In fact, as the Christmas holidays approached she realised she would be going home to London rather reluctantly.

Her boyfriend's family invited Connie to their house for an early Christmas dinner and to meet them. The day was bright and cold as Connie and her boyfriend set out. Although Connie could feel butterflies in her tummy, her boyfriend assured her that his family would love her. The lunch went very well – the food was delicious and the family warm and welcoming. Connie felt relaxed and very at home.

When the time came for dessert, Connie caught her breath. Placed in front of her was a hot, golden-brown blueberry pie! Her boyfriend's mum told her that she had made it especially, because her son had told her how much Connie had loved blueberries when living in the USA. By coincidence, the wonderful pie was accompanied by ice cream.

Connie took a mouthful and something remarkable happened: not only was she transported back to her grandmother's kitchen, surrounded by all its familiar sights and sounds, but she felt a tingling on her tongue and a deep sensation of warmth surrounding her. It was an amazing feeling and unlike anything she had ever experienced before. She could not thank this lovely family enough for their thoughtfulness and, when leaving, wished them all a Happy Christmas with a warm hug.

Arriving home in London, Connie was thrilled to see her parents and siblings again and was full of news about her new life and her college friends. When she finally got a quiet moment alone with her mum, Connie related the story of the strange events concerning the blueberry pie. Listening with moist eyes, Connie's mum said she felt sure the occasion had led to a link with her late grandmother, the love of her early years coming back with the taste. The tingling and warm sensation, she felt certain, was her grandmother in angel form, telling her that love still flowed between them. Although this was not humble pie by any stretch of the imagination, it was certainly a pie sent by the angels.

Sometimes angels offer help in the form of information, food and protection; sometimes they direct our path.

ANON

Angel Cookie

I really believe that many of us experience tastes sent to us by angels, but we simply don't recognise them. While researching this book and asking people if they had ever experienced an unusual sensation connected with food at a specific time, a surprisingly large number of people admitted they had. This would often be on special family occasions, such as weddings, christenings or even funerals, when a strong sense of love surrounded the people present.

Several years ago I was fortunate enough to be invited as a guest speaker at an Angel Day in Pennsylvania. It was a wonderfully organised day and clearly a great deal of hard work had gone into the preparations. The event was held in a large high school, the main hall of which was packed with amazing angel-themed stalls. There were wooden angels, fabric angels, glass angels – in fact, just about every type of angel fashioned from every medium you could imagine. One of the most attractive stalls, however, was the angel food stall, which had a delicious array of cakes, pies and cookies all baked in angel shapes.

Two thousand people passed through that festival in just one day and as the programme drew to a close the sensations of relief and euphoria flooded through the organisers in equal measure. It was fairly late in the evening before the stalls were finally packed away and the staff and speakers alike were invited to the home of the main organiser for a celebration supper.

It was a night I shall never forget. The atmosphere of the day flowed over into the beautiful home of the organiser, who led us through the large garden to a summer house where delicious pizza awaited us. The stars were huge and my fellow guests warm and friendly as we discussed the events of the day.

Dessert took the form of large angel cookies. As I ate mine, I was aware of a wonderful sensation on my tongue. I thought at the time this must be a secret cookie ingredient, having never experienced anything quite like it before. The evening ended with everyone holding hands in a circle under the stars and giving thanks to the angels. Once more I experienced the unusual sensation in my mouth.

This happened many years ago and at the time I didn't recognise the angelic contact. Today I would have no hesitation in recognising what was happening: I was literally eating the food of angels.

Many of you, reading this book, will have enjoyed a similar experience. The truth is that we simply have to trust – if we suspect this is a form of angelic contact then, more often than not, it is!

Never underestimate your own powers of deduction.

STEPHEN WILKINSON

∼ AFFIRMATION ∼

I open my mind to all forms
of angelic contact.

∾∽∾

Food for Thought

I would like to thank my friend the Reverend Gillian Gordon for the following excerpts from a New Church sermon on the meaning of Revelation 21:

> The water of life is a symbol for the truth of God, which is accessible to everyone all the time. In heaven our thirst will be for knowledge and understanding – and it will be there for the taking freely offered.
>
> The same is true of the Tree of life. Growing on each side of the river is the tree of life with its twelve kinds of fruit, yielding fruit all year long. And not only is there fruit but the leaves of the tree are for healing what ails you. Again, our hunger in heaven will be for love and usefulness. If we are seeking to satisfy our hunger and thirst with food and drink, we will be forever hungry and thirsty, for no amount of food or drink that goes in the mouth will satisfy our need.
>
> It is not so very different here. Food and drink satisfy the body, but no matter how good it feels to have a full stomach this does not satisfy the longings of the soul. Here on earth it is easy to think that we are being satisfied with food and drink and all other sensory delights to be had, but they only satisfy our physical needs, and our souls go on longing for love, and truth and a sense of usefulness. We must learn this here on earth and begin to cultivate a taste for things that God offers to satisfy the soul.

*The things that matter most in this world are
those that carry no price tag, for they can
neither be bought nor sold at any price.*

Suze Orman

Coffee Shop Angel

The lovely village of Haworth is set in the most beautiful of surroundings and is famous, of course, for being the home of the Brontë family. The steep little main street leads to the vicarage where the family lived and tourists pour though the house all year round. Attractive gift shops and cafés abound, but a firm favourite with visitors today is the coffee and cake shop.

Although it had always been a dream of Claire's to have the shop, this happy little place almost did not open. Claire loved to bake cakes and see people enjoy them, but everyone advised her that the shop simply would not work. There were so many other choices for food and drink in the village, they argued, that simply serving cake would be a non-starter. Nevertheless, Claire felt deep inside that this was her calling. She felt driven about the project and so, with a wing and a prayer, she went ahead with it nevertheless.

It was not an auspicious start. The crowds were not beating a path to her door and, worried that her critics might be right, Claire decided to take action. A firm believer in angels, she decided the thing to do was simply to ask the angels for help and then to trust. She baked every cake with as much love as she could muster and it appears that they must have been sprinkled with angel dust too, because trade began to pick up.

Having to economise for some time while the business found its feet, Claire's husband was forced to drive an old, battered car – something that gave Claire no little cause for concern. It looked pretty unsafe and, in an attempt to help, she gave her husband a special little brooch she treasured of the Archangel Michael. 'Humour me and hang this inside the car,' she said, adding, 'I'm sure he'll look after you.'

Her husband did exactly as Claire asked. However, the day arrived when the car was simply beyond help of any sort and Claire's husband decided sadly that it had to go to the breaker's yard. Now the old car was finally gone, crushed to a metal cube. However, without thinking, Claire's husband had forgotten to remove the special brooch, which had been hanging from the rear-view mirror. It simply had not entered his head until he told his wife what he had done with the car and saw her face go pale! In desperation, Claire rang the scrapyard, only to be told she was too late as the car and its contents had been well and truly crushed.

Weeks passed and one morning Claire reached for the wooden box in which she kept her favourite earrings. Claire loved these earrings so much that she wore them every day. The little wooden box held very few objects so the earrings were easy to find at the beginning of the day. To Claire's utter astonishment, there next to her earrings was the long-lost brooch of St Michael!

Overjoyed, she called her husband over, who stared open-mouthed at the sight. He knew that for certain he had not retrieved the brooch from the car before taking it to be crushed. It had definitely been hanging on the rear-view mirror.

Claire also knew for certain that her husband was a kind and honest man and that there was no way he would have been playing a trick on her. He was as mystified and delighted as she was to see her special little brooch returned. There appeared to be only one explanation: the angels had once more come to the rescue.

Asking is the beginning of receiving.
Through a simple believing prayer, you can
change your future. You can change what
happens, one minute from now.

DR BRUCE WILKINSON

Love in a Box

Many people use the internet to search for long-lost loved ones. There are even social websites dedicated to finding old friends, especially from school days. And amazing stories tell of those who have been reunited after virtually a lifetime spent apart. It's true that, the older we are, the more likely we are to look back and decide that we want to trace the people we once knew.

School reunions in particular can be a revelation. The people we once thought the least likely to succeed often turn out to be those who are most successful. And the opposite can be true too. The appearance of some may be changed beyond all recognition, while others hardly seem to have aged at all in the intervening years. Lesley certainly worried about this aspect when she unexpectedly received an invitation to attend a college reunion.

She opened her wardrobe, half hoping to find a wonderful new outfit she had overlooked! We have all done it – stared at our entire collection of clothes in despair, in the hope that one interesting item will appear that we had forgotten about until then. Nothing emerged, however.

Reading the invitation again, she could see that it was going to be a rather informal event – lunch in a 'middle of the road' hotel near her old college – but she still wanted to look smart. Unsure of exactly who or how many people would be there, she decided that she would have to go shopping for a new dress. Fortune was on her side as she arrived in her nearest town. To her delight, she saw that the smartest shop was holding a sale. It was almost Christmas and the seasonal atmosphere added to her mood of expectation. Some time later Lesley made her way home, clutching a shopping bag. In it was not only a lovely new dress but also a pair of matching shoes – what a treat!

The morning of the lunch arrived and Lesley began to get ready, wondering just how many of the people she had known well would be there. One name was more prominent than most in her memory: Michael. He had been a friend who for quite some time had promised to become a lot more. They had even discussed marriage at one point, but, being young and just starting out in the world, they had not gone through with it. Taking jobs in different parts of the country, they had eventually lost touch with each other completely.

Although she was now a single mum living in Britain, Lesley had married and lived abroad for many years with her husband and son. She assumed that Michael would also be married with a grown-up family by now. She wondered what his story would be. However, there was a good chance he would not be at the lunch at all, as so many of their college friends had vanished without trace, apparently.

Nevertheless looking forward to the day, Lesley set off feeling very cheerful. A loud buzz of voices reached her as she strode into the hotel lobby. No need to wonder where the lunch party might be – she simply followed the noise. As she opened the dining-room door, shouts of 'hello' and 'look who's here!' greeted her and lots of familiar faces came into view. It was lovely to see them all and Lesley began to enjoy herself immensely.

Lunch was delicious and when it was finished everyone moved into the conservatory for coffee and more chat. It was only at this point that Lesley realised Michael had not come to the reunion after all. However, just as the thought crossed her mind, the door opened and in he walked! His face had scarcely changed in twenty years and only a sprinkling of grey hair showed that so many years had passed. Having not visited the area for a long time, Michael had got lost on his way to the hotel. Everyone was delighted to see him and before long he and Lesley were chatting away like the good friends they had been, all the years slipping away.

All too soon the afternoon came to an end and people began to drift away. The lunch had been such a huge success that everyone vowed they would keep in touch and get together again. Michael and Lesley walked together to the car park, where they discovered that their cars were parked almost next to each other.

'I have something for you in the car,' Michael said.

Puzzled, Lesley walked over.

He explained that he hadn't been sure if she would be at the lunch party or not, so had left the little wrapped box in the car. Presenting it to her with a grin, he said, 'Happy Christmas!'

She opened the box and a grin spread across her face too: it was a box of chocolate-covered Brazil nuts. They had always been her favourite treat, which Michael used to buy for her on a regular basis. It had been twenty years, however, since anyone had bought them for her and her eyes began to fill with tears.

A warm, tingling sensation spread throughout her whole body and she found herself saying, 'Thank you, you're an angel!'

'Hardly,' Michael laughed, 'but I do believe they found you for me today.'

Realising they were both single, they exchanged telephone numbers and said goodbye, with a warm glow of hope between them.

The box of Brazil nuts still lay unopened on the coffee table in Lesley's sitting room months later, reminding her of the link between past and present. A box of chocolate Brazil nuts are perhaps an unlikely source of angelic intervention, she thinks, but she never doubts that they were a gift from the angels.

And with the morn those angel faces smile,

Which I have loved long since,

And lost awhile.

JOHN HENRY NEWMAN

The Food of Love

Combined together, food and love make for an irresistible recipe. Food is such a fundamental part of our daily routine, but we can use it to remind us of everything that makes life so special and precious. Here are some more simple suggestions for making each day taste a little more delicious.

* Invite friends to dinner and tell them it will cost them a hug.

* Hold a 'pudding club' night by asking all your friends to bring a dessert for everyone else to sample.

* Hold a coffee morning for your favourite charity.

* Make popcorn and share it with a child.

* Cook a dish from your childhood and taste the memories.

* Take family or friends on a country walk and pack them a delicious lunch to eat while they are out.

* Treat yourself to coffee and a slice of your favourite cake in an attractive coffee shop. You have to love yourself too!

* Make a cake – and lick the spoon; you will feel like you are six years old again!

* Ask the angels to add their love to a meal you cook for a special occasion.

* Light a candle and ask the angels to bless all those who are hungry and in need of love.

Melting Moments

When telling me her story, Frances explained that she had felt 'bone weary'. She had started out from home at 6 a.m. that morning and now, many hours later, she was tired of driving. Blessing the day she had bought a satellite navigation system, she was relieved that at least she was not lost. She was on her way home from visiting her old aunt, who lived in a nursing home some three hundred miles from the town where Frances herself lived.

According to the nursing home staff, Aunt Mabel had been fading fast as sheer old age took its toll. Frances felt feelings of guilt wash over her as she realised that perhaps she could have made her aunt's life happier if she had made more of an effort to visit her. Although Mabel was comfortable, she had admitted in the past that she felt a little isolated as the home was far from where she used to live.

Now, at only a year short of one hundred, Mabel was approaching the end of her long life. However, when Frances arrived, she had perked up amazingly. She was thrilled and grateful to see her niece.

Frances had stayed a good deal longer than she had originally intended, as she found that she loved talking to her aunt so much. They had reminisced about Frances's childhood when the two of them had lived close to each other. At the end of the visit, she promised to return very soon, realising that she needed to see her aunt just as much as Mabel needed to see Frances. The visit had triggered sensations of childhood love and laughter, which were scarce in her own life at present.

Kissing her aunt, she left for the long drive home, feeling

tired already from the emotional impact. After driving for some time, Frances felt badly in need of some refreshment and followed a sign saying 'Angel Teashop'.

'I could use an angel,' she thought, smiling as she turned her car down a quiet lane towards the small village and promised teashop.

Entering the shop, she found it deserted and was afraid that she was too late to order food. However, a smiling old lady appeared from the direction of the kitchen and asked if she could help. Frances told her she was desperate for a cup of tea and anything at all in the food line. 'I do hope I'm not too late,' she added, realising that it was turning dark outside.

'I can always look after just one more customer,' the old lady replied kindly.

In no time at all, Frances was tucking into a plate of cheese on toast and a steaming pot of tea. It was wonderful and exactly what she needed. Paying the lady, she thanked her profusely and headed for home, feeling revived.

The following weekend, Frances was determined to make the long round trip once more to see Mabel. This time Mabel was clearly very frail indeed and Frances was very happy to have made the effort, as their remaining time together was obviously limited.

Leaving the nursing home a little earlier than she had the previous week, Frances decided that she would visit the little coffee shop once more for afternoon tea. The lights were ablaze and the shop had a few customers as Frances pushed open the door. It was so warm and friendly inside that she felt very much at home.

Ordering her tea, she asked the waitress if the old lady was there that afternoon. She was met with a confused stare. 'Which old lady?' the girl asked.

Frances described her, which was an easy task because the lady had had a distinctive appearance. She explained that she had very white curly hair, deep blue twinkling eyes and a beautiful smile.

'I think you must have been mistaken,' the girl said. 'No one works here answering that description. We're all pretty young and even the owner is only in her thirties.'

Incredulous, Frances asked if anyone could have been standing in the previous Saturday, explaining that it had been rather late, past six o'clock that day.

'No, sorry,' came the reply. 'And now I'm sure you must have made a mistake, because we closed early last Saturday when we all went to the wedding of one of the waitresses here.'

To say that Frances was astonished would have been an understatement; she knew for certain that the lovely white-haired lady had served her when she needed sustenance the most. Leaving the shop, she smiled to herself as she realised exactly what the explanation was: it could only have been an angel. Looking up at the sign, 'Angel Teashop', she said thank you to her special guardian angel, who had taken care of her when she was bone weary!

All God's angels come to us disguised.

JAMES RUSSELL LOWELL

The Christmas Angel

It was one of those days in early December when it was never going to get really light. Heavy, metal-grey skies hung low over the village and a mist swirled around the trees, adding to the gloom.

Looking through the window, Rose could just about see the village Christmas tree across the square, outside the post office. The lights were switched on, trying to pierce the mist and bring a little Christmas cheer to passers-by, but failing miserably. Rose sighed; she felt at a very low ebb. As she glanced round her little room, which was totally devoid of any kind of seasonal decoration, she could feel tears prick her eyes. She had suspected that this would be the time of year when she would miss her husband the most.

Almost twelve months had passed since Frank had died suddenly from a heart attack. He had not even survived the trip to the hospital, despite the ambulance crew working hard to save him. It had been a long, painful year and now Rose had to face her first Christmas without him. Friends had been very kind, inviting her to their homes, but she didn't have the will to go and join in with their festivities. It was even going to take a huge effort to go to her daughter's house for Christmas Day. The train journey would not be terribly long, but Rose was seriously considering staying alone in her own home.

Making a cup of coffee, she settled down with her magazine, which was full of articles about the coming celebrations. Rose was just about to throw it aside when she noticed an article about Christmas past. The article was actually quite interesting and included pictures of the Thames frozen with ice thick enough to hold fairs upon it. There was even a picture of an elephant crossing the frozen river! She read how Charles Dickens's book *A Christmas Carol* is mainly responsible for the idea that Christmas should be a cold and snowy time of year. She read about churches full of worshippers and how carols became part of the traditional service. Closing her magazine, her thoughts returned to church and carols. She decided on impulse to wrap up warm and walk to the village church in order to see what time the Christmas service would be. Quickly, she pulled on her coat and scarf and ventured out into the mist.

Arriving at the little church, she paused. She was surprised to see people going inside. Why, she mused, would people be going to church at 11 a.m. on a Tuesday morning? Reading the noticeboard she saw that an hour of meditation was about to begin and she instantly felt drawn to go inside and take part. Peace and quiet in lovely surroundings were exactly what she needed.

Stepping inside she was met with warm smiles and a lady indicated that she should sit next to her. It was the most wonderful, healing hour Rose had known for a long time. Periods of silent meditation were interspersed with guided med-itations, all lovely and calming. Deeply relaxed, Rose suddenly found herself asking the angels to help her through the coming season. At the end of this special hour, everyone started to chat and Rose was invited to join them in a side room for coffee and biscuits. Feeling her spirits lift, she stepped into the little room, accepted a cup of coffee and reached for a biscuit.

Lifting the biscuit to her lips, Rose felt tears prick her eyes. These lovely pieces of confection were angel biscuits, home-made and decorated with icing and glitter. Instantly Rose was transported to the days when she would make these biscuits with her daughter and the warmth and fun they had shared as a family, eating them on Christmas Day. The very taste brought back a sense of love and she realised that, no matter what she faced in life, love survived. She still had wonderful memories of happy family life.

Walking home through the mist, she silently thanked the angels for their timely message and marvelled at how a simple little biscuit could turn a miserable day into something joyous.

The conclusion is always the same:

Love is the most powerful and still the most unknown energy of the world.

Pierre Teilhard de Chardin

A Few Festive Facts

The Christmas carols we are familiar with today come mostly from the 1800s. Carolling, however, is an old English term meaning 'to sing joyfully'. Eating mince pies, and gingerbread too, dates from the Middle Ages when Crusaders to the Holy Land developed a taste for exotic spices. The pies were originally made with meat, of course.

Poinsettia plants are relative newcomers to the Christmas celebrations. They were introduced by the United States Minister to Mexico. He heard a story about a Mexican child who was too poor to give a present to the baby Jesus and who had no way of leaving money in the poor box on Christmas Eve, as was the local custom. The boy prayed for help with this dilemma, and then he saw a beautiful red flower growing at his feet. He swiftly picked the plant and presented it to the church, where it adorned the statue of Christ. To this day the flower is known in Mexico as 'Flower of the Holy Night'. The American minister took a specimen of the plant home with him each Christmas and so began the Western tradition of taking poinsettias into churches and homes at Christmas. Who was this minister from the United States? Why, Dr Joel Poinsett!

Flame of angels burning bright,

Lift our spirits in the night,

Bring us joy and happiness,

Reach us now our hearts to bless.

DOROTHY MADDISON

Tree of Heaven

If you can use a scented candle for this meditation, that would be perfect. However, a regular one will also do. Light your candle in a quiet moment when you are alone and feel comfortable. Calm your thoughts and breathe deeply for a short time.

In your mind's eye, see yourself walking through a long arbour of orange trees. The scent is heady. The sun is warm on your back as you slowly walk between the beautiful trees. There are no people to be seen or noises of any description; all is perfectly quiet and calm.

On the ground in front of you a wicker basket lies directly in your path. Pick up the basket and carry it down the avenue of trees. As you reach the end of this beautiful walkway, the trees open out onto a magnificent vista of valleys and mountains, which are snow-capped and shine in the sunshine. The sky is deep blue and the scent and scenery make you feel as if you have peeped into the Garden of Eden.

A figure appears before you. Dressed in white, it is a young man, smiling at you with a gentle twinkle in his eyes. He makes a sweeping gesture with his arm towards the trees and it is clear that he wishes you to pick some of the fruit.

Take a large orange from the tree and hold it to your nose. Smell the wonderful fragrance of the skin and appreciate the wonderful intense colour of this fruit. Sit down on the grass and peel the orange, enjoying the intense aroma as the peel lifts and the flesh appears. Slowly eat the delicious fruit, tasting the sunshine in each mouthful.

The young man slowly turns and, walking a little distance from where you sit, he suddenly faces you with a smile and simply fades away. You realise at once that this fruit has been a gift from an angel. As you slowly make your way back the way you came, along the arbour of orange trees, a feeling of spirituality pervades the entire orange grove.

Become aware once more of being alone in your room and slowly open your eyes. Blow out the candle and stretch your limbs slowly. If you have an orange in your home, lift it from the bowl and smell the aroma. Picture the angel and his smile. Know that all wonderful fruit is a gift and give thanks.

Orange Cakes

Here is a heavenly dish! This recipe makes approximately sixteen cakes.

> 2 oz (50 g) self-raising flour
> 3 oz (75 g) margarine
> 5 oz (150 g) granulated sugar
> grated rind of a small orange
> 1 egg
> 4 tablespoons milk

Preheat the oven to 375°F/190°C/gas mark 5.

Place the dry ingredients in a large baking bowl or the bowl of a food processor. Rub the margarine into the flour and sugar until it resembles breadcrumbs. Blend slowly if using a food processor. Add the grated orange rind, then beat the egg into the milk. Gradually add the milk and egg, mixing thoroughly, and then drop the mixture into a greased muffin tin or grease-proof paper cups. Bake for fifteen to twenty minutes. When cool, dust the cakes with icing sugar and decorate with confectioner's orange slices.

* ❋ *

Angels are in a way
a seasoning to make God more palatable.

JULIA CHILD

Today I give thanks for the blessing
of food and drink.

⟿⟿⟿

How to Satisfy Spiritual Hunger

As we have seen, virtually every notable occasion in our lives has a type of food associated with it. There will be many different smells and tastes that transport you back to particular times when you felt incredibly happy. Could a happiness-provoking taste for you be linked to your childhood? Perhaps you used to arrive home from school to find freshly baked cakes on the table, then you would taste one and feel that all was right in your world. Or maybe your special food memories are linked to sampling a new fruit or food for the first time, perhaps while you were on holiday abroad? Is your private moment of taste-heaven connected with the first time you cooked a meal yourself or for someone special? Maybe it's held within a glass of champagne at your wedding or that of a close friend? A simple cup of coffee, perhaps, reminds you of an important occasion and someone special you shared it with.

Whisk yourself back to an especially lovely day in your life. It could a day on which you ate a delicious ice cream on the beach, baked with children or had a celebratory slice of cake – whatever evokes a happy memory for you. Close your eyes and 'feel' the food or drink on your tongue. Allow an inner sensation of fulfilment to envelop your senses. You may promise yourself that in the near future you will cook or buy the foodstuff that is filling you with such happy memories right now.

Recall the warm glow of that time when you were so happy and realise that happiness is attainable still. If you felt such sensory happiness once, you can experience it again. Keep the glass always half full! Put love into your recipes and the angels will do the rest!

A good cook is like a sorceress
who dispenses happiness.

ELSA SCHIAPARELLI

Smell the Coffee

I am sure you will be familiar with the expression 'wake up and smell the coffee', which urges us to become more aware and awake to the world around us. Think about your own life. What might be amiss in it? Take stock for a moment to consider what you have not yet tasted in your life.

When we feel that life is mere routine – that our day has nothing to offer but more of the same – it really is time to wake up to all the wonderful flavours that life has to offer. What we need is something 'outside the box', for want of a better expression; this is when we need to act on impulse and not have our entire week planned in advance.

Is there a new place near you, perhaps a little café or art gallery, that you have wanted to visit? If you are feeling stuck in a routine, now is the time to go. We all need food for the soul and the imagination. Lauren Bacall, the famous American actress, once wisely said, 'Imagination is the highest kite one can fly.' We all need stimulation for the taste buds of the mind. This is our life, not a rehearsal and, if we allow it, it's a life that can be full of wonder.

There is of course no denying that a certain amount of routine has to be part of most people's lives. Earning a living, for example, means that there will be a certain amount of adhering to a timetable for most of us. But if we use our imaginations and ingenuity, we can all schedule time to 'fly our kites'.

Wake up and really smell that coffee: it will inspire your day and your life.

A little of what you fancy
does you good!

MARIE LLOYD

Dreaming of Angels

During my years of researching angelic intervention I have found that dreams are often a source of angelic messages. Sometimes the dream may contain a warning or coincide with an event happening to someone close to us. I have come across many reports of people who have dreamed of a loved one lying seriously ill in hospital, only to find the following morning that the loved one has in fact died in hospital during the night. There are also dreams about people from the past, who haven't been seen for many years, yet who shortly afterwards reappear in the dreamer's life.

Often the sight of an angel in a dream serves as a form of comfort or encouragement during a particularly difficult time in life. I have to say, however, I have encountered only a few stories of dreams of angels that involve food. One amazing story was the dream of two brothers in the USA who were told by an angel to bake muffins! I tell the story in full in one of my previous books, *An Angel Healed My Heart*. In short, the dream inspired the two brothers to become very successful business-men. Having never baked a thing in their lives before, they took the dream's advice and their muffins are now sold the world over.

I was particularly interested, therefore, when a young lady approached me at one of my workshops with an angelic dream experience that related to food.

✳ ✳ ✳

Ambrosia for Amanda

To say that Amanda was confused about her path in life would have been putting it mildly: since leaving school five years earlier she had dipped her toe into many a prospective career but had been totally disillusioned every time. Her parents had paid for several courses that they hoped would lead to a career for her, but now their patience was wearing thin. Each time, Amanda would begin a course with great enthusiasm, only to find a few months later that she hated it totally.

Now her family and friends were urging her to seek advice or to think long and hard before wading into yet another course. Initially Amanda had laughed this off, convinced that something would eventually capture her imagination and use her talents, even though she was unsure what exactly those talents consisted of! As time went on, she became increasingly distressed about her situation and was feeling very low physically and emotionally. Meeting with a good friend one day for coffee, she melted into tears and was rather surprised when her friend said, 'Have you tried asking your angel?' The thought or, indeed, the very concept of angels had never entered her head but, the more she thought about it, the more interested she became. Her friend told her that simply asking her own angel for help had several times made everything clearer for her.

For a day or two Amanda pondered the idea of angelic help and one night before she climbed into bed she found herself saying aloud, 'Please, angel, if you are there can you help me?'

On waking the next morning, she was amazed that she could recall a very vivid dream. In the dream, a beautiful angel had appeared to her. Holding out a hand containing what appeared to be a gift, the angel smiled – encouraging Amanda to take the offering. Reaching out, Amanda took it: it was a small loaf of bread. Totally puzzled, Amanda saw the angel indicate that she should eat the bread. The taste, she recalls, was quite wonderful and, eating it slowly, she watched as the angel faded.

Taking her notebook from the bedside table, Amanda wrote down the details of her dream. It was at this point, she told me, that it felt like someone had opened a window for her. She realised at once that the thing she enjoyed most of all was baking and cooking. Suddenly it seemed as though it had been obvious all along – this was something that she loved, and in which she was also talented.

The dream marked the start of her catering course and when we met she had been qualified for a while and was working for a well-known and successful patisserie. Blissfully happy and fulfilled, she now thanks and consults her angel on a daily basis. Truly manna from heaven!

It is the simple things in life
that make living worthwhile, the sweet
fundamental things such as love, and duty,
work and rest and living close to nature.

LAURA INGALLS WILDER

* ❋ *

In Praise of Good Taste

Here is another little exercise that will help you to welcome the angel of taste into your life.

First, treat yourself to your favourite item of food or drink. Are you passionately fond of special bread or a particular cheese, ice cream or a chocolate bar? Perhaps you sometimes crave a cream cake but deny yourself the pleasure? Maybe there is something you particularly like to drink on special occasions.

Then, I want you to choose a day and time when you will be alone with your special treat. Make this a time in which to reflect on how fortunate you are and how many people in this world have only the basics to survive upon or literally nothing at all to eat.

Enjoy your treat, then promise yourself two things: firstly, that you will make a donation to a charity aimed at easing world poverty and, secondly, that you will treat a friend or your family to a little indulgence too. This time, enjoy your treat with others, savour the taste and the company, and give thanks for the gift of taste.

CHAPTER 5

The Touch of an Angel

There are, of course, many different ways in which we can be touched. The most obvious is a physical connection. However, we can also be touched emotionally or, indeed, spiritually. We may be moved by the sights of nature and by the words and deeds of people. Music and art both touch the soul in different ways and make our spirits soar. The touch of an angel, however, has to be the most amazing sensation of all. Wonderful descriptions abound of angelic hands felt on the shoulder, of soothing angels stroking hair, of tingling sensations and the feeling of being encircled by wings – yet these are just a few of the myriad ways in which angels can touch humans. I have come across stories of people being physically lifted off their feet by an angel's touch and being moved from the path of danger. There are others that recall unseen hands holding onto a person's arm or shoulder and people being literally being supported by angels when their own physical energy fails them.

Touch is very important in all our lives and a lack of it can render a person very sad indeed. I recall a minister friend of mine who was a tall, charismatic man who showed a great love for everyone he met. One Sunday morning, while he was shaking hands with members of his congregation, he became aware of a tiny old lady hovering in the doorway. When everyone else had left, she came forwards again and so the minister asked if everything was all right. She replied, 'I was holding out for a hug.'

My friend laughed, conscious of the fact that he did indeed often give her a hug on Sunday mornings but had omitted to do so that day. He bent down and gave her a big bear hug. She laughed too, but then said, 'Thank you. This is the only time I ever have physical contact with another human being.'

He was very touched by her reply and it led him to think about how many lonely people there must be who long for a caring touch. The experience gave him a new perspective on the expression 'out of touch'.

A moment's love can, and shall,
make the world perfect.

SRI CHINMOY

The Power of the Gentlest Touch

Who cannot fail to be moved by the touch of a little child? When little arms are outstretched and you lift the child into your arms, it is like the touch of an angel. Similarly, a much-loved pet sitting on your lap or bounding up for a stroke or a pat are examples of the importance of touch.

How lovely on a hot summer's day, is the touch of a passing breeze on the face? Have you ever stood at the water's edge on a beach and felt the tide lapping around your feet, encircling them and then retreating? It is a magical sensation and never fades no matter how old we become.

All these wonderful experiences bring the angels closer to us in our daily lives. All are part of the heart-warming experience of touch.

I was listening to the voices of life,

chanting in unison.

JOHN TRUDELL

In the Arms of an Angel

December 2008 was the coldest December in the UK for a long time. Temperatures fell below zero for long stretches and the pavements were proving rather difficult to negotiate, especially for the elderly. The TV weather programme explained that temperatures would be a couple of degrees warmer for those living by the sea, which Edith found amusing. Although she lived by the coast, she certainly did not feel any degrees warmer than the rest of the country. Instead, the ice was thick and dangerous outside.

For several days Edith stayed in the warmth of her little cottage, peering out at the ice and snow, keeping warm and feeding herself from her supplies. However, as the days passed, she realised that she really would need to venture forth to buy fresh food and indeed to breathe a little fresh air. A very active lady despite her eighty-five years, Edith did not enjoy being cooped up for days on end. As she climbed the stairs to bed on her fourth day indoors, she vowed that she would be courageous and go out the following day, whatever the weather.

The following morning dawned bright and beautiful, with deep blue skies. The sunshine made everywhere sparkle and after breakfast Edith picked up her bag, wrapped herself in warm clothes and set out to visit the shops. The bitterly cold air took her breath away as she stepped out of her little cottage, but the scene was so lovely that Edith felt her spirits rise.

As she crossed the promenade she gazed out to sea, enjoying the view and the sun sparkling on the water. People were walking their dogs on the beach and many others had ventured out to enjoy the view, although they were walking briskly in the cold. All in all, it was a glorious day and Edith was determined to enjoy it.

After a moment looking out to sea, Edith felt the cold penetrate her coat so she turned to cross the road and walk on to the shopping centre. What exactly happened next will remain a mystery, but Edith assumes a patch of ice must have made her lose her footing. Suddenly she felt her legs disappear from beneath her and she hurtled towards the concrete. Recalling in an instant the stories she had read of dying and of seeing your life flash before your eyes, Edith now saw her immediate future flash before her: broken bones, hospital and confinement. She groaned, waiting for the inevitable thud.

Astonishingly, no thud came! Instead a pair of hands caught her and gently placed her on the ground. She sat in shock and in sheer wonderment that someone had been on hand to rescue her.

A couple walking their dog appeared at the top of the steps that led from the beach. They rushed to her aid. 'Are you OK?' they asked, helping her to her feet.

Edith looked around but there was no one behind her. 'I'm fine,' she replied shakily. 'If it hadn't been for the kind soul who caught me as I fell I'd surely have broken several bones.'

The couple with the dog stared at her in confusion. 'No one caught you,' the man said. 'We saw you fall and rushed up the steps to help – you were completely alone on the promenade.'

Saying nothing except to thank them for their kindness, Edith turned and slowly made her way back across the road. Arms had held her – she knew that for certain – and if no one could see those arms and, indeed, the promenade had been deserted when she glanced behind her, then she had the answer. Although she had been a firm believer in angels all her life, Edith couldn't ever recall having had an angelic experience before. However, now that she was in her later years and needed them most, the angels had caught her in their arms.

An Angel Embrace

Relax into your chair, light a scented candle (ideally one with the fragrance of the sea), and concentrate on your breathing for a moment or two. Take some deep breaths and, with each one, relax a little more into the chair.

Close your eyes and visualise a beautiful beach. The sand is white and fine, the sea a turquoise blue, crystal clear and gently lapping the shore. Walk slowly to the water, feeling the fine sand between your toes and the warmth of the sun on your back.

The air is filled with the scent of tropical flowers and birdsong. You are quite alone yet perfectly safe and comfortable.

Approaching the water you marvel at the pretty white tips of the gentle waves and how blue the sky is over your head. Wade into the water, feeling the warm silky sensation on your skin. When the water reaches your waist, lie on your back and gently float; enjoy being rocked in the warm water. Looking up, you notice the sky is cloudless with just a large white bird circling overhead. As you float feel the cares and worries of everyday life drift away.

Turn over now from your back and slowly begin to swim to shore, enjoying the warmth of the sun and the sparkling light all around you. As your feet touch the sand once more, walk from the sea and sit on a rock to take in the lovely scene.

As you sit there, you feel the sensation of arms encircling you and you know that this is your angel, protecting and guiding you.

Slowly open your eyes and become aware of the room as you blow out the candle. Remember the touch of the angel on your shoulders and know that you are always within her reach.

The Value of a Hug

One of my favourite authors is the American Unitarian minister Robert Fulghum. His books are quirky, funny and full of wisdom. Perhaps his most well-known book is the international bestseller *It Was On Fire When I Lay Down On It*. No matter how often I read this book, it makes me laugh and marvel at the wisdom it contains.

Fulghum writes amusingly about a great 'hugging plague'

that broke out in his church one year. A Greeters Group decided this was the way to meet people as they arrived in church to make them feel wanted and loved. Robert explains that the 'huggers' got out of control and hugged people a little too vigorously. When things were quiet they would even resort to hugging each other. Not everyone wanted to be hugged and the point he is making is that perhaps moderation in all things is the way to go!

Perhaps we should ask someone first if they would like a hug before launching ourselves at them. Or we could hug them mentally and send them love with our thoughts. However, there should be no holds barred when it comes to hugging our loved ones, so hug away and enjoy every one! A hug is a wonderful way to connect with someone else physically and emotionally.

Everyone entrusted with a mission is an angel.

All forces that reside in the body are angels.

MOSES MAIMONIDES

The Kiss of an Angel

In chapter two, The Sound of Angels, you will have read the lovely story of Laura and her grandmother, Clarice. Angelic contact with Laura has been such a blessing for Clarice, helping her through her grief at losing the little girl.

One day, a friend casually asked if Clarice had ever attended a reiki meeting. Knowing absolutely nothing about reiki, Clarice asked for more information and eventually decided it might be very interesting to learn how to become a reiki practitioner herself. The whole experience was a revelation for Clarice, as she discovered that, by helping to heal others, her own healing process was enhanced. In many respects, it was an emotional day when Clarice came to be attuned to level one of her reiki healing practice.

Meditation was to be part of the day and Clarice felt calm and relaxed as she settled in for the session. During her state of deep meditation, with her eyes closed, a vision appeared to her. She observed what she initially believed to be an archway with a brilliant light shining through the centre. However, concentrating on this beautiful scene, she realised that the archway was in fact two huge angel wings. The feathers of these wings were composed of the purest, dazzling white and Clarice was filled with wonder.

She began to wonder why she had been given this privilege but the answer came swiftly. A figure walked through the wonderful wings. It stood immediately in front of them and somehow even appeared to be attached to them. Adjusting her eyes to the scene, Clarice saw with joy that this figure was none other than her dear granddaughter Laura!

She walked towards Clarice. Although she had the same long blonde curls and beautiful smile, she somehow appeared to be a little older. Softly calling to her 'Nana', Laura came closer and her face became a blur. But then Clarice felt Laura's fingers touching her hair and her beautiful light butterfly kisses all over her face.

At this point the guided meditation was reaching its conclusion and Clarice heard the tutor's voice saying that she should return to the present. It was with great reluctance that Clarice allowed herself to resurface. So emotional had the experience been that she found herself in floods of tears. They were, however, tears of happiness. She knows that the wonder of that moment will remain with her for the rest of her life.

* ✳ *

Many theologians argue that when children die they continue to grow in heaven. The eighteenth-century philosopher Emanuel Swedenborg states that the angels take care of little ones until they become young adults in the heavenly world. As I write these words, I glance at the calendar a friend bought me earlier in the year. To my astonishment I see that it is 'Grandparents' Day' and the anonymously written quote for the day reads: 'Allow yourself to sense the soothing feel of an angel's touch'!

Discover the Power of Touch

There are many simple yet powerful ways to awake the power of touch in your life. Once you are more comfortable with touch and all that it brings, you may find that it is easier for the angels to communicate with you through this sense.

* Give someone you love a hug on a regular basis.

* Treat yourself to a pamper session. Aromatherapy will 'touch' several senses at once.

* Book a hair appointment and experiment with a new hairstyle while enjoying the luxury of someone doing your hair for you.

* Stroke your cat or dog lovingly – if you don't have a pet, borrow one!

* Join a dancing group and enjoy the close encounters.

* Go for a swim and feel the soothing sensation of the water on your body.

✳ ✳ ✳

Every blade of grass has its angel that bends over it and whispers, 'Grow, grow.'

THE TALMUD

Mind the Gap

Many young people today take a 'gap year' between school and university to travel and hopefully broaden their minds. Often this involves working abroad for a charity or simply travelling with companions, working their way around the world. The experience can be wonderful and sometimes even a little daunting.

A few years ago, Anna joined a couple of friends on a gap year in Australia. It was hard work at times, as they struggled to find jobs to pay for their accommodation and living costs. However, the beautiful locations were a bonus and life was exciting for the girls. After several months in Australia, they moved on to New Zealand and once more began the search for jobs and accommodation. Only a few weeks passed, however, before one of Anna's friends announced that she was extremely homesick and decided to use her return ticket to fly back to England.

The two remaining friends were very sad and the little party appeared to have lost some of the sparkle it had set out with. However, the girls decided to carry on and caught the ferry to South Island, having spent some time in the North. Unfortunately, they chose a rather wild and windy day to make the crossing and soon Anna was feeling decidedly unwell.

Finding a seat on deck, she closed her eyes and longed for the boat to reach the dock. Soon she fell into a deep sleep, rocked by the movement of the waves. Waking with a start, she realised that the boat had docked and that passengers were streaming ashore. Grabbing her rucksack, Anna looked around for her friend and was confused by the fact that she was nowhere to be seen. With increasing concern, Anna dashed around the ferry but could see no sign of her friend. Finally, she came to the conclusion that her friend must already have left the boat and she stepped down the gangway close to tears.

People were queuing in all directions but there was no trace of Anna's friend to be seen. Panic swept over her and she felt at a loss as to what to do next. It was simply inconceivable that her friend would leave without her and yet here she was – totally alone.

Placing her rucksack on the ground, she sat on top of it and, almost without thinking, closed her eyes and asked her guardian angel for help. Looking back, she had no idea why she did this; it had never occurred to her to do so before, but then she had never felt as alone as she did now. At once she felt a hand on her head, stroking her hair, and a warm sensation flooded all through her body.

Anna quickly opened her eyes and looked around, thinking it must have been her friend's touch, but there was no one within reaching distance of her. Realising that this must have been her angel's response, she felt decidedly more cheerful. She purposefully lifted her rucksack and strode to the nearest line of people. Walking to the head of the queue, she found her friend, who was white-faced and on the verge of tears. After giving each other a good hug, it emerged that Anna's friend had also walked around the deck, looking for Anna, and had become disorientated as soon as the boat docked. She too had searched frantically for her friend but they had simply missed each other, both searching in different directions. The friend became convinced that Anna had left the boat and she thought she would hurry after her. So there had been a big misunderstanding all round.

No doubt they would have met up sooner or later, but Anna says the sheer panic and distress she felt would be difficult to describe and her angel's touch was a huge comfort at that time. At no other time since that day has Anna had a similar experience, but it has given her confidence for life, she says. She says that she now knows for sure that, should she ever need her angel, she only has to ask.

> *Everything we call a trial, a sorrow, a duty,*
> *believe me that angel's hand is there.*

FRA GIOVANNI

Reaching Out of Our Comfort Zones

As we grow up it is important for us to learn to become self-reliant. Increased confidence can come at any age when we dare to pursue new ventures and experiences. However, the hard part is knowing just how much or indeed how far to push our adventures and boundaries. We are here on earth but once, and life is wonderful – offering many bounties to the brave. Yet we do not always need to travel the world in order to enjoy our share of these wonders, as many lie close to home.

To begin with, we might begin by being just a little more adventurous on a weekly basis, building up our confidence until we feel ready for bigger things. We can try to be less concerned about the opinion of others and trust our own. Seeking constant assurances from others can stifle our own initiative, so throughout our lives we need to learn to take ourselves forwards. When we do, we will be rewarded by the inner strength this brings.

I have a friend who retired from her job. She had been looking forward to rest and relaxation, only to find herself feeling slightly depressed and bored. Never one for taking steps alone, she was at a loss as to what to do about the situation. One morning, as she walked past the local library, she spotted a notice for a local book group. She was at once attracted to the idea and at the same time filled with fear at the thought of joining a group of people where she knew no one. She has no idea what finally gave her the impetus, but she went along and joined the group, heart in mouth but determined. It proved to be the best move she ever made: not only did she make lots of lovely like-minded friends, but the group had a strong social life too. Together they enjoyed meals out and frequent trips to the theatre. The experience turned my friend's life around. As the astronaut Neil Armstrong famously said: 'One small step…'!

He who deliberates fully before taking a step,

will spend his entire life on one leg.

CHINESE PROVERB

*This is my life
and I am living it
to the full.*

Desert Angel

I first met Dr Peter Ruppel in Munich, where I had been a guest speaker at an Angel Festival. After my talk, Dr Ruppel came to chat to me and told me an amazing story. He had been blessed with an angelic encounter in the most unusual of places and circumstances.

On reaching retirement Dr Ruppel and his wife had decided that they wanted to travel. This was the perfect time in their life to see the world and off they went, full of excitement and anticipation. Eventually they found themselves in South America, where they hired a car in which to go exploring. They drove through several countries and terrains until one morning they decided to set off into a desert. The road became more and more empty as they drove deeper into the desert landscape. Eventually they realised that they had hadn't seen another vehicle for a long time.

It was at this point that the worst possible thing happened: the car broke down! Not mechanically minded by any stretch of the imagination, Dr Ruppel climbed out of the car to check for the obvious signs of engine failure. He could find nothing wrong and no amount of tinkering and turning the engine worked; the car had well and truly given up the ghost!

Calmly, he and his wife assessed the situation. It appeared grim. They were on a deserted road, in the middle of a desert, and had seen no vehicles of any description for a long time.

For reasons he cannot explain, Dr Ruppel said he felt oddly calm, even though he would usually have been beside himself with anxiety. Standing next to the car, he assured his wife that all would be well. After a little while, a dot appeared on the horizon, coming towards them, and Dr Ruppel watched as the shape grew in size until he could identify it as a truck. He said it reminded him of the scene in the film *Lawrence of Arabia*, where the approaching camel grows ever larger. Eventually the truck reached them and stopped.

The driver jumped down from the cab with a cheery hello. There was something quite unusual about this man, whose calm air and strangely ethereal appearance made the couple feel safe and secure.

'Open the hood of the car,' he ordered gently, and to Dr Ruppel's amazement he simply placed his hand on the engine, as if blessing it!

'Try the engine now,' the man said. Doing as he was bid, Dr Ruppel started the car engine, which immediately burst into life!

Without another word, the man climbed back into his truck and drove away, while the astonished couple were left open-mouthed, marvelling at the event. Even though they set off straightaway in the same direction as the truck, with the intention of saying thank you to the driver when they caught up with him, they couldn't see anything ahead of them. The straight road was clear and flat, and they could see for miles, yet there was no sign of the truck.

This very practical, down-to-earth doctor and his wife both came to the conclusion they had been helped by their guardian angel that day in the desert. Touched by the angel in a very unusual way indeed.

*Seekers are offered clues all the time
from the world of the spirit.*

Ordinary people call these coincidences.

DEEPAK CHOPRA MD

Healing Star

Light your candle, sit in your most comfortable chair and relax. Take several deep breaths and feel yourself sink into the chair.

Picture yourself on a warm summer evening, walking slowly up a gentle slope that leads to the top of a hill. From the top of this hill you can see for miles, a glorious view of beautiful fields and streams flowing in the valley bottom. You sit down on a warm, flat rock and take in the lovely scene spread out below you.

The fragrance of night flowers reaches you as the evening draws in and dusk falls. You feel safe, warm and comfortable as you watch the landscape gradually darken. One by one, sparkling stars appear in the dark sky and you catch your breath at the beauty of the scene.

The worries and problems of your day fly through your mind but fade in the moment. Suddenly you gaze in sheer amazement as a shooting star streaks across the sky and appears to pass almost within touching distance of you. You feel instinctively that this star is sent by the angels to take your cares away.

One after the other, shooting stars cross the sky and reach you, inviting you to place your worries and problems into their light. Then they shoot off into the darkness, taking away all your cares with them. Speaking out loud, say what each of your problems is and, as you say them aloud, place them onto the passing star and watch them leave.

Feel the sense of relief as the sky lightens once more and you find yourself sitting in daylight on the top of the beautiful hill. The sun rises and the warmth and light fills your heart and mind. All your cares have been lifted away by the shooting stars and you can walk freely, with a light heart, down the path.

Become aware of your room again, your comfortable chair beneath you, as you stretch your arms and legs. Once more, take some deep breaths. Blow out your candle and thank your angel for the wonderful stars.

Our lives are like the course of the sun.
At the darkest moment there is the promise
of daylight.

THE TIMES

❋

Be thou a smooth way before me,

Be thou a guiding star above me,

Be thou a keen eye behind me,

This day, this night, forever.

If only thou, O God of life,

Be at peace with me, be my support,

Be to me as a star, be to me as a helm,

From my lying down in peace,

To my rising anew.

SAINT COLUMBA

How to Keep in Touch with Yourself

Are you really in touch with yourself? And, if you aren't, how can you reach out to touch others? Here are some simple ways to activate the principle of touch in your own life.

* Look in the mirror each morning and tell yourself you have the power to achieve.

* Have you lost touch with a once much enjoyed talent, such as music, art or sport? Research how to rekindle your enjoyment in this area by joining a club or taking a course.

* Picture in your head what it is you really want and

behave as though you already have it. Having self-belief is half the battle.

* Have you ever wished to contact an old friend, having regretfully lost touch with him or her? Make the effort to rekindle your friendship and enjoy having them in your life once more.

* Schedule some 'me time' into your week and make sure that you make the most of it – without feeling guilty!

* How long is it since you bought yourself a little 'gift'? Make today the day – you deserve it.

* Remember a day in your life when you felt truly happy and in touch with all aspects of yourself. Re-run the memory and know that you will achieve such happiness again.

* Tell yourself that this is your time. Believe and you will achieve.

* * *

*The greatest gift that you can give yourself
is a little bit of your own attention.*

Anthony J. D'Angelo

Wings of Desire

The leaden grey sky seemed so close overhead that Helen felt she could reach up and touch it. Even though it was only early October, it felt like winter had arrived with unseemly haste. The weather suited Helen's mood, however. She had felt weighed down with cares for some time and simply could not shake off the feeling of foreboding. It was not as if some overwhelming tragedy had taken over her life; rather a series of small disappointments had accumulated and were dragging her spirits down.

A job that Helen felt sure would be perfect for her had eluded her at the interview stage. A relationship that she had had high hopes for sadly came to an end and then her travel plans had to shelved when a close relative became seriously ill and needed her attention permanently. There appeared to be little time for fun in Helen's life and she was only too aware of the fact that her negative attitude and depressed disposition was driving her once supportive friends away.

Reaching for a book about positive thinking, she made a cup of coffee and decided she would look for a little advice within the covers. However, the encouraging advice about going for a walk, swimming with friends or tidying her room and belongings only seemed to make her feel worse.

Suddenly lightning flashed across the grey sky, making Helen jump and triggering her tears. As they flowed down her face uncontrollably, Helen realised that this was the first time she had cried about her situation and once she began it seemed impossible to stem the stream. How she wished her parents were still alive – she knew that a shoulder to cry on and a hug would have gone a long way to helping at the moment. But sadly Helen had lost her parents some time ago.

At last her tears subsided, the storm outside had moved on and there was a little sliver of blue visible in the sky. Taking a few deep breaths, Helen resolved to try to tackle her problems and, instinctively, she said aloud, 'If I have a guardian angel, please help me.' Her own words came as a huge surprise to Helen, for to her knowledge she had never even thought about angels, guardian or otherwise, before in her entire life!

Imagine her amazement at what happened next...there was a definite sense of arms cradling her in a hug and a warm sensation washed through her entire body. The sensation was one of being encircled by pure love and she felt a sense of complete awe and wonder. There was no doubt in her mind that her own special angel had heard her and responded. It felt as though a special valve had opened up in her heart, allowing love and optimism to flow in. She suddenly entertained hope for the future in a way that she had not done for many months.

The sky outside Helen's window was now the clearest blue, brightening along with her mood, and she gave thanks to God for her miracle. Not a particularly religious person, before or indeed after this experience, Helen nevertheless is a firm believer in angels!

To comfort and to bless,

To find a balm for woe,

To tend the lone and fatherless,

Is angels' work below.

W. W. HOWE

Angel at the Bridge

Sheena wrote to me from Edinburgh with her account of angels rescuing her one dreadful night. Life had been extremely difficult for Sheena for a long time and she felt that she could endure no more. At her lowest ebb, she believed that no one – not even her family – understood the depths of her despair. As she sat there, listening to the radio, she suddenly heard the well-known country and western song 'Ode to Billy Joe' in which a young man throws himself off a bridge. The lyrics resonated with Sheena and she resolved that this would be the way out for her too.

One bitterly cold night that winter, Sheena decided to jump off the Forth Bridge. Running down the railway line on the bridge, she was aware of the station master calling out to her and trying to reach her. However, so determined was she that she quickly reached a point she knew was extremely high. In an instant she had leaped over the edge. She fell a terrifyingly long way, down and down, before landing on firm ground. Her first thought was that both her legs must be broken but – amazingly – she was definitely alive.

It was at this point, Sheena says, that she felt a hand rest gently on each leg and heard a voice say softly, 'I love you.' This, she is convinced, was a voice from God and she knew at that moment she would eventually walk again.

Despite surviving the fall, Sheena was very badly injured and an ambulance rushed her to hospital. The stay in hospital would be a long one but the medical staff found it difficult to believe she could have survived such an incident at all. Some time later, as her mother sat by her bedside, Sheena told her about the voice and the hands she had felt on impact, convinced that an angel had broken her fall. It was a profound spiritual encounter and helped Sheena to realise that her life was a precious gift. To this day, she feels sure that God and his angels ensured her survival that dreadful night.

Touch and Go

We may make an effort to keep in touch with our family and special friends, yet so often we lose touch with ourselves. Caring for others is essential and admirable, but we must also stay in touch with our own needs. Perhaps we may need a daily reminder of what chores should be done and what can in fact be jettisoned! Are we going through the motion of daily duties without looking closely enough at what might not be essential?

I am going to give you some advice that may make you groan – in fact, I can almost hear you say, 'I have been told this dozens of times before…' Maybe so, but believe me it works; I am referring, of course, to the act of writing a daily diary. Making an effort to record events and feelings each day can be hugely beneficial and will help you in a very short time to get in touch with what you really feel and to realise what you most need to be in touch with. So treat yourself to a beautiful notebook and perhaps even decorate it in an appropriately angelic manner, with stickers, cut-out pictures and ribbon.

In your Angel Book, you can make some simple notes in answer to the following questions. Firstly, do you have enough space? Are you losing touch with the essentials in your life because of the sheer clutter that surrounds you? Take a good look at your answers.

Nothing appears to be clear or distinct if we find ourselves feeling hemmed in. You don't have to wait until spring to have a thorough spring clean, so have go now: throw away those unwanted items and enjoy the space created. Whittling down personal detritus to the bare essentials will remind you of life's important issues. Give yourself room to 'swing a cat' (a term from sailing days of old, the cat swung being the 'cat-o'-nine-tails' whip, not the poor domestic moggy!); as a result, you will have a clear space and a clear head.

Being in touch with yourself is essential for happiness and fulfilment. Give it a try – and literally touch and go!

― AFFIRMATION ―

*Today I open up my heart and
mind to let God and his angels
touch my life.*

Soul Touch

We might assume that everyone enjoys the sense of touch, but sadly this is not so. Many medical conditions such as nerve damage after a trauma or illness can render our sense of touch void. A friend of mine has a benign tumour that sits directly over a nerve, blocking sensation to the whole of his arm. Often just a small part may be affected, but some people cannot feel touch in large areas of their bodies. Stroke victims may lose sensation down the whole of one side.

Sadly, there are cases of paralysis in which virtually no part of the body has sensation. A young lady I met in the USA some time ago had been involved in a terrible car accident. Lying in bed, she could feel nothing from her neck downwards. Mercifully, in her case, after weeks of intense therapy her sensation returned and she is now fully recovered. During her time in hospital, however, she frequently saw an angel standing at the foot of her bed, or could occasionally smell a wonderful heavenly fragrance. Despite her struggle she told me that she thanked God daily for his protection and for sending his angels to her. Her belief in angels certainly helped her regain health and strength.

When life presents more challenges than
you can handle, delegate to God.

He not only has the answer, He is the answer.

TAVIS SMILEY

*Today I will stay in touch
with my angel.*

∞∞∞

A Birthday Gift to Remember

Many of us may fulfil the ambition of a lifetime on a significant birthday. As the celebrations approach, we tell ourselves it's 'now or never' and we seize the day. Hot-air balloon rides, a day driving a racing car or a special trip are all popular pursuits on such occasions.

For Stefan, however, his lifetime's ambition was to fly a helicopter. A successful businessman, as he approached the milestone age of fifty he was determined to buy himself this wonderful gift. The process of achieving his ambition to fly was far from simple. The training, the purchase of the helicopter and the paperwork involved proved to be a complicated and time-consuming affair. At last the day really did dawn when Stefan could fly his very own helicopter.

The thrill and delight on Stefan's face was lovely to see, but his wife, Sarah, understandably had her own worries about this development in their lives. It looked like a highly dangerous form of transport to Sarah and she struggled to remain positive about it for her husband's sake.

Stefan's maiden flight was to be from his home to an airfield in Liverpool where he had received his training and where he longed to show his friends his beautiful new helicopter.

Preparing to leave, Stefan said goodbye to Sarah, who suddenly had a premonition that all was not well. A strongly spiritual lady and a firm believer in angels, she felt as though she had been given a warning. Not wishing to spoil this pleasure for her husband, however, Sarah kept as calm as possible but pressed upon him a medal and a cross, both blessed with holy water, and a prayer card asking the angel Michael for protection. Stefan took the items from her and promised to place them prominently in his helicopter. At last Sarah began to feel calm and she wished him a happy and enjoyable flight.

Watching the helicopter take off from an upstairs window, Sarah looked out onto the field they owned behind their property. Up went the helicopter and soon it was in the air. Almost instantly, Sarah realised that there was a serious problem as the helicopter started to rock violently from side to side. Then, to Sarah's horror, it fell from the sky, plummeting to earth like a stone!

Running downstairs as fast as her legs could carry her, Sarah made for the door leading to the field. The sight that met her eyes on the other side made her heart leap into her mouth – the helicopter was completely on fire. Her only thought as she raced onto the field was how on earth would she be able to get her husband out of the burning inferno. But then she realised that a miracle appeared to have taken place for, standing alone and completely unhurt, at a very safe distance from the burning wreck, was Stefan! Rushing to her husband in disbelief and a state of shock, Sarah promptly fainted.

Sometime later they discussed what had happened and Stefan told his wife that almost instantly on take off he felt that there was something seriously wrong. He had fought to keep control but there was no response from his controls at all. Despite his efforts, he found himself dropping towards the earth at a sickening rate. At this point he was totally mystified as to what could have happened next. One second he was hurtling towards the ground, the next he was standing looking at his machine on fire.

A passing man, who was walking his dog and witnessed the crash, said, 'It was like watching a film – he simply flew out of the helicopter door.' Certainly, Stefan could not have climbed out of that burning helicopter unaided and it would have been impossible to escape instantly, at such speed. He could recall nothing about his exit from the machine, only remembering how he stood watching from afar.

Sarah is positive that the angels saved her husband that day. The incident was reported widely by the media, who were also at a loss to provide a different or rational answer. Sarah, however, has no doubt that her premonition and invoking the angels that day brought her husband home safely.

See, I am sending an angel ahead of you
to guard you along the way.

EXODUS 23

Experience Tactile Happiness

Sensations of touch often remain very clear in the memory. If we think back in our own lives, we may be surprised by how many memories of touch are linked to joyful thoughts. We may recall sunny memories from childhood, such as being hoisted onto an adult's shoulders to see a special event, a goodnight hug and kiss, or a tap on the shoulder from a teacher expressing in touch as well as voice, 'Well done.' Other happy memories of touch may come from times when we are a bit older, perhaps when we held hands with a loved one or cradled a baby in our arms for the first time. In terms of your own memories of touch and happiness, perhaps you can recall a congratulatory embrace from a dear friend, dancing with a partner on an important night or lifting a child onto your lap in order to read a story. All these moments produced inner contentment that you can recall at will today.

To do this, simply close your eyes and feel that special moment and memory of touch – and know that this moment may be replicated, that you can be happy in that way again. Should you ever doubt this, close your eyes once more and summon up the sensation of that loving touch.

If we are prepared to open ourselves up to the distinct possibility that we may be touched by an angel, then there is every chance it will happen. Many people have experienced an angelic tap on the shoulder accompanied by a sensation of love, stroking of the hair or even a spiritual hug with angelic arms encircling them. Allow yourself to be touched in every sense of the word.

Hold the fleet angel fast until he bless thee.

NATHANIEL COTTON

Hug a Tree

You may have heard some people referred to (none too kindly) as 'tree huggers'. This implies they are at the very least eccentric. However, getting in touch with nature has long been a method of finding peace and spiritual fulfilment. There has always been a link between the natural world and otherworldly realms.

Have you ever wondered, for instance, where the expression 'touch wood' comes from? This came from the medieval practice of knocking on the trunk of a tree and asking the tree spirits who lived within it for help. If the help proved to be forth-coming, people would once more go to the tree and knock on the trunk to say thank you to the spirits.

In ancient times, specific trees or woodlands were often known as sacred places and used as sites for worship. Touching stones and shells, or bathing in certain rivers and waterfalls, all involved connecting with your inner spirit and reaching out to the spirits in nature. This form of worship was especially true for indigenous peoples, for whom the earth and all its natural treasures were sacred. Canyons and huge trees such as redwoods are to many people nature's own cathedrals.

Following recent excavations, historians now believe that the inner circle of blue stones at the famous Neolithic site of Stonehenge was believed to have healing properties and that people would travel from mainland Europe simply to touch them. The examination of bodies buried near the ancient site has confirmed that these individuals travelled long distances to be there and the nature of their bone injuries also suggests that they believed touching the blue stones would result in their conditions being healed. Belief in the healing power of nature, be it wood or stone, clearly goes back a long way.

When a man plants a tree, he plants himself.

JOHN MUIR

Tree-mendous

'It probably goes back to childhood,' Richard said, 'but I've always had a deep fascination with trees.' He explained how there had been a wonderful tree house in his garden while he had been growing up and how he had always felt a strong affinity with any kind of tree.

Visiting country parks or stately homes when he was older, Richard found that he was particularly intrigued by very old trees, wondering just how many people had stood beneath their branches over the ages. He wondered what kind of lives those people had led and what history had unfolded there. He would ask himself, like thousands of others gazing up at such trees, 'I wonder what they would say, if only they could talk!'

A great love of the outdoors meant that Richard was a keen walker and, as a university student, he joined the climbing club. There was a summer trip to Scotland to go walking and climbing after the term had finished, and Richard could scarcely wait.

At last, their studies behind them, the group of friends set off. Loaded down with climbing equipment, they also took tents and cooking utensils, planning to sleep and eat outdoors as much as possible. The weather was kind and setting up camp that first night was idyllic. The warm night air made cooking under the stars a real adventure.

Richard wanted a break from the soul-searching that had dogged him during term time and longed for several of his problems to melt away during the trip. His studies weighed heavily on his mind for, after two years of his course, he had begun to doubt his choice of subject, but dreaded broaching this with his parents. How could he expect them to continue to support him morally and financially after wasting – in their eyes, he was sure – two whole years?

The night wore on until at last, in the small hours, the friends started to climb into their sleeping bags. Soon Richard was aware that everyone else was sound asleep, but much to his annoyance sleep would not come for him. He found his worries returning and spinning around in his head.

Crawling out of his tent, he looked around and saw it was a beautiful night. Overhead the stars were clear and twinkling. It was a long time since he had seen the stars look so large and bright. Here, away from city lights, they filled the night sky. He pulled on a sweater and walked a little distance from the group of tents and his sleeping companions. It was then that he noticed a little way ahead of him a huge tree, its branches silhouetted against the sky.

Reaching this wonderful tree Richard felt like a child once more and wanted to climb into its branches. Leaning against the trunk, however, he found himself telling the tree his problems, just as he had done all those years ago as a child. It felt wonderful and soothing, and on impulse he turned and gave the lovely old tree a hug. To his astonishment, tingling sensations ran through his arms and he felt a sense of peace envelop him. Staring at the tree, he asked himself if he had imagined it but he knew this was not the case.

Some time later, Richard managed to confide in his mother about the experience with the tree. She didn't laugh as he had expected she would, but gave him one of my books to read.

I received an email from Richard, who asked if I considered signs and symbols in nature (as had been mentioned in that particular book) to extend to spirituality in trees. 'Could angels be reaching out to me from a tree?' he asked. I had no hesitation in assuring him that angels reach us in whatever way we find familiar and acceptable – whatever the medium, if you feel an affinity for it, then the angels will happily use that medium to contact you.

That night was a turning point, Richard confided, and the beginning of a personal spiritual journey.

*A yew is as important as Durham Cathedral
and a hell of a sight older!*

DAVID BELLAMY

* ✻ *

The tree of Peace has four white roots
extending to Earth's Four Corners.

Anyone who desires peace can follow the roots
to their source and find shelter under
The Great Tree.

DEGANAWIDA (THE PEACEMAKER)

Appreciating the Sense of Touch

At specific times throughout the year you might enjoy adding tactile objects to your home altar or sacred space. What objects do you have that may be particularly pleasing in a tactile way? You might come across the bark of a tree, an autumn leaf or a piece of moss that still feels springy and warm to the touch. On holiday, you might come across a string of smooth and cool glass beads which feel lovely to run through your fingers. Perhaps you pick up a stone from a beach or riverbed, which could be particularly rough or smooth. Maybe you add a piece of material such as silk or velvet or fine wool? For fun you could add some bubble wrap and enjoy popping the bubbles! If you have a cat or dog in the house, why not take them with you to your special space and give them a loving stroke? Tactile pleasure is a gift we should never take for granted.

Time to Take Stock

Before moving on to the final chapter in this book, which is about our sixth sense and angels of the soul, now is a good time to look at what barriers might be preventing us from experiencing angel contact.

In comparison to the other five physical senses, the sixth sense of intuition is possibly the most difficult area in which to recognise angelic intervention. This sense needs nurturing and we need to pay close attention if we are to recognise the voice of our inner angel speaking. The promptings of our inner angel may be so subtle that time and again we dismiss them as mere coincidence or the product of our imagination.

Personally, I feel that there is no such thing as 'mere coincidence'; all coincidences are meaningful, even if the meaning is not always immediately obvious.

Are there certain aspects of your life that prevent you from receiving your inner angel's guidance? Do you need to clear your spiritual decks in order to be able to appreciate its presence?

Having cleared our external personal space, we must now turn our attention to our inner space. Could a cluttered inner space be preventing us from having a clear view of life? Do you suspect that 'must do' tasks are clogging up your days and, on inspection, are not so important or relevant to your wellbeing after all? Give yourself a moment to take a quick look at the areas that might be holding you back and clouding your peace of mind and happiness. (You can jot your answers down in your Angel Book, if you have one.)

✳ Do you feel constantly tired? Could there be an obvious reason why this is the case? Are you overcommitted to projects that require too much of your time and energy? Would it be sensible to whittle these down? Are you failing to delegate where appropriate?

✳ Are you guilty of trying to please everyone except yourself? You are vitally important in this equation – your health and strength must be a priority or you will fail to please anyone. Focus on the most important issues and leave the rest.

✳ Have a clear-out! Starting with your personal belongings… Are you holding on to things that you no longer need for no reason other than you like to hoard? Sort out the essentials and throw the rest away. Does the same thing apply at the office? Reduce that pile of paper sitting on your desk or in the 'in tray' and you will feel terrific. Vow to keep it that way.

✳ At the beginning of each week, take your diary and schedule in spare time for yourself – and stick to it!

✳ Enjoy a fun activity with a good friend or two. If the activity involves movement, such as dancing or swimming, so much the better.

✳ Meditate each day whenever possible. Meditation helps clear the mind and will slow you down when you need it most. Slowing down is sometimes as important as speeding up!

* Write a list of the most important people in your life, the most important activities and the aspects of your life you enjoy most. Concentrate on these.

* Realise that you are a talented and beautiful person – because it is true: we all have our own talent and type of beauty.

* Plan some pleasurable events each month with people close to you. That way you will always have something to look forward to.

Give yourself a break! You deserve it.

CHAPTER 6

Angels of the Soul

*The Universe provides the answers
to our questions.*

*We can hear them only if we open our hearts
and tune in our souls.*

JUDITH LEVENTHAL

*S*oul angels are very special indeed for they are the angels within us all. We each have an inner angel and the more we exercise our inner angel qualities the more powerful they will become. Importantly, the more we recognise those qualities in others, the more they will grow in them too. It reminds me of the children's song 'Magic Penny', which says that love is like a magic penny – the more we spend the more we have.

It is through our very soul that angels contact us most frequently, but unfortunately it is precisely this form of communication that is most often dismissed or ignored. We all too often misinterpret that 'still small voice' and shrug it off as imagination or coincidence, when in fact, if we were to concentrate and listen to it, its messages would become more frequent and clear.

'I knew that would happen' – at one time or another, most of us will have experienced knowing what another person is about to say before they actually speak, or we will have realised who is ringing before we answer the phone. Similarly, there will be times when our inner voice gives us a message or a warning but we simply refuse to believe it.

Listening to your inner voice, or soul angel, is something that requires practice but – like all practice – the more we listen the easier it becomes. If we learn to trust this contact it will bring us the wisdom, advice and the comfort we may need so badly. So many times people ask me if a certain feeling, sensation or sign was angelic in nature. Deep inside they already know it is, but simply wish to have that confirmation from me. We must trust and, if at times we misinterpret signs, well, it is very unlikely that we will have lost anything in the process.

An angel can illume the thought and mind of man by strengthening the power of vision and by bringing within his reach some truth which the angel himself contemplates.

SAINT THOMAS AQUINAS

* * *

Soul Connection

It was to be an annual conference with a difference! Robert was very excited as he packed his case for the trip. His company had pushed the boat out on this occasion and the delegates would be staying at a beautiful hotel in a stunning coastal location.

However, the icing on the cake for Robert was the fact that his managing director had told him that promotion was coming his way and that the directors would be interviewing him in the coming days. Robert knew deep inside that he was good at his job and that he gave one hundred per cent in terms of commitment. The promotion would be a reward for his hard work and results.

It felt good to know that his superiors appreciated his efforts. Since leaving university, Robert had been focused on making his life a success. He had bought his own small house and was beginning to enjoy the rewards of his efforts at last.

Climbing into bed that night, he set his alarm for a dawn start, knowing it would be a long drive and aware that he had to collect other members of his team along the way.

The morning dawned bright and crisp; it was a perfect early autumn day and the trees were just beginning to change colour. Closing his front door behind him, Robert walked down the path. His spirits were high. As he steered his car out of the driveway and onto the road he was thinking about the quickest way to get to the home of the first of his colleagues.

Suddenly, a very strange sensation came over him and he was aware of an inner voice telling him to drive to his mother's house. 'Nonsense,' he thought – it was simply his imagination.

The voice, however, was insistent. Although it was inside his head, it was clear and strong. 'Drive to your mother's house!' it urged once more.

What a dilemma! If Robert did take the road to his mother's house he would be driving in completely the wrong direction and he would certainly make himself late. Traffic would already be building on the route to the coast and the last thing he wanted was to arrive late at this special event. His colleagues would not appreciate being kept waiting either...could he really alter his plans because of a voice in his head? However, the feeling that he had to obey only became stronger and, in a sudden moment of decision, he sped off towards his mother's house.

On arriving, he entered her house with his key. All seemed quiet and well. 'How stupid am I?' he wondered bitterly, feeling instantly angry with himself for having delayed his journey.

His mother was clearly asleep in bed and he thought he would just pop his head around the bedroom door before heading off again. Slowly opening the bedroom door in order not to disturb or alarm her, Robert peeped inside. With horror he discovered that she was not in bed at all – she was lying unconscious on the bedroom floor.

He rushed over to her, taking his mobile phone from his pocket and calling an ambulance. Within minutes the ambulance crew had arrived and Robert accompanied them to hospital. Phoning his colleagues, he apologised and asked them to leave without him.

Some time later, after his mother had been attended to, it emerged that she had suffered a heart attack and that Robert's timely arrival had saved her life. It is essential to get heart attack patients to hospital within the hour if they are going to have a good chance of recovery, and this was what had had happened.

Today, Robert is overjoyed that he obeyed his inner voice and that he literally saved his mother's life. He shudders to think what might have happened, had he thought the voice was just his imagination and ignored it.

Telling me his story, Robert says he had no idea that there was such a thing as an angelic intuitive intervention but, having read several books on the subject since the event, he feels overwhelmed at having received such a blessing.

The lovely ending to his story is that his mother has made a full recovery. Oh, and, by the way, he got his promotion too!

As soon as you trust yourself

You will know how to live.

JOHANN WOLFGANG VON GOETHE

Tinkerbell

Tinkerbell was fading fast. The predominantly young audience at that afternoon's performance of *Peter Pan* sat watching, holding their breath, eyes wide. We were instructed to 'clap our hands if you believe in fairies'. I watched as the little ones around me clapped furiously and then saw them smile broadly as Tinkerbell's light started to glow once more. The children's love and belief had saved her.

I thought about angels and pondered how, if we all showed a stronger belief in them, they would light our lives ever more powerfully.

A belief in a higher source literally enhances our lives. It bestows not only happiness, but physical bounties too. In recent years studies have revealed that worshippers with a strong faith, who attend services, live on average approximately seven years longer than those who do not. It would seem that their strong belief in a higher power that protects them and guides them leads to their enjoying a richer and healthier life.

Trust and believe in your angels, they will literally be the inner light of your life.

Follow what you love!…Don't deign to ask what 'they' are looking for out there. Ask what you have inside. Follow not your interests, which change, but what you are and what you love, which will and should not change.

GEORGIE ANNE GEYER

The Power of Self-Belief

When talking about belief we must remember that self-belief is also vitally important. We may ask God and his angels to step in and help us in many ways, and indeed they will, but we need to believe in ourselves first.

Tell yourself that you are capable of your heart's desire and act as if it is only a matter of time before your goals are achieved – it is not a matter of 'if' but 'when'.

Intuitive life coach Gary Quinn, with whom I have co-authored a number of books, always advises his clients to: 'Fake it, till you make it!'

The angels can help, but you must not leave all the hard work to them. Get to work on your self-belief and together you will achieve.

> *Until you see yourself as successful,*
> *no one else will see you that way. Choose to*
> *see yourself as a happy, talented and lucky*
> *person. Act, talk and behave like the person*
> *you want to be, and you will become*
> *that person.*

> FIONA HARROLD

How to Hear Your Soul Angel

Everyone has an inner angel, even if they don't realise it. To connect with your inner angel, there are a few simple things you can do.

✳ Tell the angel you are listening! Simply say that you are open to messages and will endeavour to become increasingly aware of them.

✳ Choose a quiet moment in the day, light a candle, be still and open your mind to the fact that your angel is ever close.

✳ Next time you have the sensation of 'knowing something' without being told, jot it down in your Angel Book or a notebook for future reference.

✳ When you feel emotionally moved by a wonderful piece of music or nature in all its wonder, say thank you to your angel.

✳ Treat yourself to a soul-nurturing day doing the thing you enjoy most. Visit an art gallery and marvel at the paintings or sculptures. Attend a concert playing the kind of music that makes you feel happy. Or treat yourself to a day at the seaside or in the country, breathing in the fresh air and giving yourself space.

✳ Should you find yourself thinking about someone without apparent reason, contact that person; you may discover they need you or indeed you may need them – and your angel is pushing you to discover which!

✳ Exercise an angelic, unselfish quality. Give someone you love a gift for no apparent reason. Make a donation to a worthy cause that you have thought about but never acted upon. Give someone who lives alone the gift of your time with a short visit.

✳ Realise that there is more to life than your job and making money. We all have to survive but people and relationships are equally important.

✳ The next time you see someone looking attractive in

any way, tell them – you will see their inner angel in the smile you receive in return.

✳ Tell the people you love just how much you care about them and feel the glow.

* ✳ *

*When you find yourself declaring that
absolutely no way can you take time off,
that is exactly what you need to do.*

JENNIFER LOUDEN

Heart to Heart

The first time anyone hears the voice of their inner angel, their immediate reaction is usually, 'Did I imagine that?' It is difficult to describe the sensation of internal communication that is not exactly a voice, not from external sources and yet not quite telepathy. Nevertheless, the communication is quite real and is probably best described as an activated 'sixth sense'. The person experiencing the communication may take a little time to adjust but, if they stay with the experience, they will realise that, without a shadow of doubt, they are hearing the voice of an angel.

So often the voice of an inner angel takes the form of a loved one who has passed away and the message may be very important. Once the message and reassurance have been delivered, in many instances the inner angel will never contact the person quite so directly again. It is as if as the angel's job has been done.

This was certainly the case for Sue, whose emotional journey in recent months had been challenging, to say the least. It had been a very painful year for Sue, as she had endured the deaths of three immediate family members: her mother, father and brother. Everyone faces loss and pain at some point in their lives but for Sue the grief of this threefold experience was extreme.

One of the saddest aspects to this story was the fact that Sue's mother had been suffering from the effects of a stroke and was in a very confused state of mind when Sue's father and brother passed away. Her nearest and dearest were further distressed by realising that Sue's mother did not really understand what had happened. The final blow for Sue came when her mother herself died. Perhaps the fact that she had been unaware of Sue's grief had compounded the loss for her.

A string of events soon after losing her mother brought Sue to the home of her friend Joanne. Joanne was a student of reiki and as part of her course she had to practise her healing on several people and file reports on her treatments to her teacher. It occurred to Joanne that she could ask for a donation for her treatments and give this to a cause close to her heart, namely Cancer Research.

Knowing that Sue had lost three members of her family to the disease and knowing also that reiki treatment might prove beneficial to Sue, she called her friend and invited her to take part in her treatment programme. Sue, as you can imagine, was only too eager to be involved and went along for her appointment, pleased to support her friend and the worthy charity.

The treatments proved relaxing and healing for Sue. She had not felt calm like this since the death of her loved ones. On her third visit, Sue relaxed instantly and felt herself open up to the full sensations of the therapy. Joanne was a wonderful practitioner and a spiritual atmosphere surrounded them both.

Suddenly, Sue became aware of a tingling sensation in her arms and legs, totally unlike anything she had ever experienced before. She lay there, totally confused as to what it might be. She then sensed a presence and an internal communication, rather like telepathy but clearly and without doubt the voice of her mother. The message was wonderful and simple: at last Sue's mother understood everything, she was whole again and at peace. Sue was not to worry – everything was clear and resolved. It was truly an amazing experience and put Sue's mind at total rest.

Slowly, the treatment came to an end and Sue opened her eyes to see Joanne looking at her in amazement. 'Did you feel anything during that treatment?' Joanne asked and, when Sue described the tingling, Joanne smiled broadly and said that she too had felt it; so powerful was the sensation that it had also been transmitted to Joanne.

It was lovely for Sue to be able to share what had happened and to tell her friend how she had been contacted by this wonderful means of soul connection. She felt relieved and blessed to have experienced it. Certain that this will not happen again, Sue knows that the message her mother wanted to pass on has indeed been understood and that without doubt she initiated a true 'heart to heart' with her daughter.

*Love is the energy through which
all people and things are made, You are
connected to everything in your world
through love.*

BRIAN L. WEISS, MD

* * *

*Meditation is a time of quiet, when the mind is
freed from its attachment to the hysterical
ravings of a world gone mad. It is a silence in
which the spirit of God can enter us and work
his divine alchemy upon us.*

MARIANNE WILLIAMSON

Connecting with the Heart

Make sure you will not be disturbed for a while and sit comfortably in your favourite chair. Relax, holding your hands palm upwards loosely in your lap. Take several deep breaths and consciously sink deeper into the chair.

Picture the very centre of your heart where you see a tiny pink rosebud, petals firmly closed. This rosebud represents love and your inner angel. As you gaze into your heart the rosebud begins to grow until it is a large pink rose the same size as your heart. Slowly the petals start to unfold and the rose opens to reveal a tiny angel smiling at you and sending love.

Feel the warmth of her love as she continues to grow. Soon the angel is standing in front of you and the glow of light and love is filling the room. This process of growth continues until the angel hovers over your house, spreading love and light to all below.

Picture this process as the angel grows to the size of your town or village, filling the sky above with her love. The entire country is now under the protection of your angel and still she grows. Reaching to the very edge of space your angel's love covers the whole world.

Imagine just how far the love from your heart has gone, encircling the globe with light and love. As you picture this wonderful sight you notice that the angel is once more changing, but now she is growing smaller.

From the edge of space she contracts until she covers the whole country, your town, your house and then once more stands in front of you. Finally she returns to the very centre of your heart and the pink petals of the rose close over her until once more there is a tiny bud inside your heart.

This small rosebud, containing so much angelic love and light, will always be with you and you will be able to open it at any time.

Be aware of the chair beneath you and your breathing, how your chest moves with each breath. Once more, take several deep breaths before opening your eyes and having a very good stretch.

Two Souls

Researching the family tree has become a fascinating pastime for many of us today. There are lots of websites dedicated to helping these searches and there are even popular TV series about people tracing their family histories. Could it be that we are looking to the past because many of us feel rootless in today's society? Today, it is not uncommon to move around the country – and even the world – to live and work, and so the extended family has given way to the nuclear family. Somehow we are missing the ties that once bound us to family.

Whatever his unconscious motive, William felt a strong desire to trace his ancestors and so, armed with a rudimentary family tree, he set off for Germany from his home in London to try to fill in some gaps on the branches.

Finding to his delight that the records in Germany were very clear, thorough and easy to access, William was soon very satisfied with the results he had unearthed. When he established that one of his ancestors had come from a small village in the Rhineland, he decided to end his trip by travelling down the Rhine to find the little place.

It turned out to be a delightful little town, with an old world charm, and William decided to stay for a couple of days to look around. On the morning he was due to catch the riverboat to travel back down the Rhine, he bought a coffee and sat looking out on the pretty scene while he waited for the boat's arrival. The café was busy and a young woman asked if she might share his table. Only too happy to oblige William said yes and they fell into conversation. It soon became clear that the girl was English and that she lived in London. Further conversation revealed that not only did she and William live in the same part of the city but only a mile or so apart.

At this point the ferry arrived and William stood up to collect his belongings, sad at leaving this lovely girl so soon. To his delight, however, she got up to catch the same boat and explained that she would be taking the same route home to London as William. Happily they travelled together and – as you may have guessed – on arriving in London they agreed to stay in touch.

Today, they are engaged to be married. They intend to be in touch for the rest of their lives and hopefully add branches to their own family tree!

*Just when you think you are alone, take one
more step, walk one more block, for just
around the corner, there may be new
friendships waiting to begin.*

JUDITH LEVENTHAL

~ AFFIRMATION ~

Today I give myself the gift of love.

Spiritual Synchronicity

This is an amazing story about an event that happened to Sarah, whose husband almost lost his life in the helicopter crash as described in chapter five. I really think that Sarah is naturally close to the angels. She appears to have an open channel to them, which is kept flowing through the strength of her belief and which means that she is subsequently heard by them.

Shuddering as she recalls what took place one night in her home, Sarah explains that the whole experience was truly terrifying and it is a testimony to her faith in angels that she coped so well.

Living in a rather isolated place has its compensations but also presents its own problems at times. The night in question Sarah was home alone with her baby son, who was only weeks old. Her husband Stefan was working and had phoned his wife to check that all was well. He also warned her that he would be late home that night. Sarah wasn't at all worried and, switching off the light, she climbed into bed with her young baby boy asleep in the cot beside her. It wasn't long before she fell into a light doze. Like all new mothers, she slept with one ear ready to hear the slightest noise from her baby.

Some time later, Sarah was woken by the sound of footsteps outside the bedroom. Much to her shock, the door burst open and three men raced into the room, shining a torch into her face and yelling at her to remain exactly where she was. Rigid with fright, Sarah doubted she could have moved very far anyway, but became extremely distressed when she was forced to lie face down and felt her mouth and arms being taped firmly. However, most terrifying of all was the sight of a shotgun being thrust into her face. Amid the confusion Sarah found herself saying silently, 'Someone help me, please.' It was a silent cry from the heart in those desperate circumstances.

The men began to search the house, presumably looking for money and valuables, when suddenly – for no apparent reason – they ran down the stairs, jumped into their car and fled the scene. To Sarah's huge relief, the next person to enter the bedroom was her husband. It transpired that, even though he was extremely busy at work and should not have left for some time, an inner voice had urged him to go home immediately. So insistent was this sensation that he had jumped into his car, a powerful vehicle, and sped back as quickly as he could.

Stefan and Sarah eventually decided what they believed must have happened. The three men had possibly heard and then seen the approaching car. Due to the speed with which Stefan had come up the driveway, they had assumed it was the police. Maybe they thought the house had a direct alarm that they had failed to detect and that this had resulted in the police car arriving so swiftly.

It was of course a huge relief for Stefan to see that his wife and baby were relatively unhurt. Sarah had never been so pleased to see her husband. They agreed that some form of spiritual synchronicity must have been at work that night and that their soul angels had sent out the alarm call. Their soul angels must have been working overtime. Thank goodness Stefan did not dismiss that inner call but acted instantly.

I wonder how many times people have heard an inner voice urging them to act and have decided to ignore it – with grim consequences. Our inner angels are always at hand; we simply must take heed of them.

The angels are the dispensers and
administrators of the divine beneficence
towards us. They regard our safety, undertake
our defence, direct our ways, and exercise a
constant solicitude that no evil befall us.

JOHN CALVIN

Animal Intuition

Some people are so close to their pets that they seem to have a spiritual connection with them. Stories often reach me of people who have seen their pets once they have passed away. The bond between pet and human may be so close that the sense of loss can be intense when the pet dies. However, the connection would often seem to survive.

For one family, the grief was felt keenly by every member when their much-loved cat died. I met Roswitha at the Angel Festival in Munich, where I had been invited to speak. It was a wonderful weekend, held in an old converted monastery, and I met many interesting people. At the end of the first day, Roswitha came over to chat and told me a heart-warming story about her cat Gina.

One morning, before setting out on holiday, Roswitha, her husband and children were saying goodbye to Gina as she sat on the balcony of their house. However, as Roswitha stroked her, she suddenly realised that something was wrong with the little cat as she was having trouble breathing. Cancelling the holiday immediately, Roswitha rushed Gina round to the vet's surgery.

The vet tried his very best to help Gina, but despite all his efforts her health continued to fail. An anxious week passed before Gina was taken to see a specialist. The news was the worst possible. He told them that the illness was very serious indeed and there was nothing he could do for her.

The following day Roswitha's children gently stroked Gina and talked to her lovingly. Gina had always replied to them with little mews and had always interacted closely with the family. Now she seemed to understand the situation perfectly, as well as the fact that she was much loved.

The morning came when Gina was so weak it was obvious that she only had a very short time left. She was failing fast and would clearly have to go to the vet to be put to sleep later that day. With great sadness the family said goodbye to her. Kneeling by the cat, Roswitha stroked her and told her that by the time evening came she would be in heaven, where her mother would be waiting for her. Gina looked up and answered her; it was almost as though she understood every word.

Her final journey to the vet's was a very sad one for everyone and as they drove along Roswitha's husband said to Gina, 'Could you please send a sign that you are safely on the other side?' The vet examined Gina once more in the hope that there might be something he could do that would save her, but during the examination Gina died.

Gina was brought home again, where she was buried in the

garden in the shade of her favourite tree. As they stood there, Roswitha's husband said that the previous night he had experienced an odd dream in which another cat had come into the garden to help Gina die. Everyone went back into the house feeling terribly sad – she had meant so much to them all.

Twenty minutes later, Roswitha and her husband walked out onto their balcony, where the most wonderful sight met their eyes. Stretching from the tree under which Gina had been buried, in a wonderful huge arc that reached all the way to the distant mountains, was a spectacular rainbow. They caught their breath and Roswitha's husband said, 'I didn't think she would be able to send the sign so quickly!' It was a wonderful sight and a natural sign from the heavens that brought them comfort that evening.

Another odd incident made them think that Gina might be sending them a further sign. The very next day a strange neighbourhood cat strolled into their garden and started to slide down the children's slide, an action that it repeated several times. The family believed it was another signal that Gina was safe in heaven. The strange cat apparently still visits them!

Be genuinely concerned and love
all God's creatures,
your love will have its own reward.

DONNA LUCAS

Be at Peace with Yourself

There are many things you can do to help make it easier for your inner angel to contact you. Perhaps the most important thing to do is to be at peace with yourself, so that your angel can easily make its small, quiet voice heard in your everyday life.

* Concentrate on what really matters in life. What do you really care about and what do you want to experience more of? Focus on the things that mean the most to you.

* In your Angel Book, write a list of everything you feel grateful for.

* Look for the rainbows in life. The smallest glimmer of sunshine spreads colour across a stormy sky.

* Give yourself a 'soul gift' such as an uplifting book you have long been meaning to buy.

* Meditate regularly on the beauty that surrounds you. Even if you live in the middle of the city, there will be beautiful things that you can reflect upon – such as the lights reflected in puddles, flower boxes and the trees in parks.

* Treat yourself to a print of a favourite painting or a piece of original artwork (maybe even a child's drawing) to hang in the room where you meditate.

* Write an 'angel request list' of six things you want to happen in life. Reflect on it and then trust the angels to deliver.

* Buy yourself a bunch of flowers and place them in a vase where you shall see them and appreciate them.

* When alone in the house, sit down with a cup of coffee (or tea if you prefer) and play your favourite piece of music.

* Appreciate the animals in your life and garden – and give thanks for them.

— AFFIRMATION —

I love myself, knowing that, when I do, I find it easy to love everyone else.

A Spiritual Hotline

I have always believed that coincidences have spiritual origins. With certain people we are close to, there is definitely a 'soul synchronicity'. A very close friend in Los Angeles is constantly amazed at how we connect, often with amazing synchronicity. Similarly, significant family events will often coincide with my phoning or e-mailing those concerned.

Recently my friend was undergoing treatment for cancer. It had been a long journey and throughout it she had been positive and brave. The final stages of her treatment were approaching and everyone desperately hoped that this would mark the end of chemotherapy for her, although there was a real possibility that another course of treatment would be necessary.

However, I had no idea exactly what date she was due to be seen by the consultant or, indeed, what would be discussed during her next appointment. Yet my friend was on my mind all that day and I felt a strong urge to contact her.

The following morning, I lit a candle and asked the angels to be with her. I then sent an e-mail, asking how things were going, and explaining that she was prominent in my thoughts. She told me later that she read my e-mail on the very day she was due to leave for the appointment.

Happily, the doctors were thrilled and amazed to see that the results of various tests showed that my friend was completely clear of cancer. No further treatment was necessary, which was wonderful news.

I have received stories from all around the globe about synchronicity, further proof (if any were needed) that many people experience this phenomenon. Sometimes, the level of synchronicity is so amazing it simply takes my breath away.

*Life is not measured by the number of breaths
you take, but by the number of moments that
take your breath away.*

ANON

Star of Bethlehem

It had felt like a long winter, with grey skies and a great deal of rain. The garden looked pretty dismal too as Beryl vowed to tackle it that morning. When she set to work, her first job was to take down the hanging baskets and replant them in readiness for the spring.

The plants in the baskets all looked dead – apart from one little shoot that looked suspiciously like a weed. Nevertheless, Beryl thought she would plant the shoot at the bottom of the garden, just in case it turned out to be something else. As she dug a hole for the little scrap of life, she thought that it was probably a waste of time, but she felt compelled to go ahead and plant it all the same.

Some weeks later, life became a struggle for Beryl. She had been feeling unwell and was awaiting a hospital appointment to undergo tests. Fearing the worst, she felt terribly anxious and low as the day of the appointment approached.

Looking through her kitchen window just prior to leaving for the appointment, Beryl was confused to see a white globe peeping through the greenery at the bottom of her garden. Many times a day, while working at the kitchen sink, Beryl looked out onto her garden and yet she had never seen this white cluster before.

Drying her hands, she walked to the end of the garden and gasped in astonishment at the sight before her eyes. A large ball of white flowers flourished on the shoot she had thought to be a weed. Not only were the flowers beautiful, but they were of the variety Star of Bethlehem – her late mother's favourite flower. There could be no clearer message for Beryl: her mother was close and all would be well.

The tests were duly carried out and Beryl remained calm the whole time. Indeed, only a short time later the results arrived, stating clearly that nothing serious was indicated. It was the most wonderful news.

It is still difficult for Beryl to comprehend how the Star of Bethlehem plant came to blossom so profusely when only the day before there had been nothing to be seen in the spot but the little green shoot. Many times Beryl has felt her mother's presence but this time the beautiful sign from the garden provided absolute confirmation that she was being watched over by her.

*I trust the signs from nature as a
message from the angels.*

∞∞∞

Soul Signs

When I am speaking to audiences, the subject of 'signs' will frequently be raised. Many people can recall a time in their lives when a robin appeared at a particularly significant moment, a flower blossomed (as for Beryl in our last story), or a butterfly landed close by: these seemingly small events may carry a much greater emotional charge. On these occasions, the individuals concerned may have fleetingly wondered if the event was an angel message but, as we have seen in some of these stories, so often that thought will be dismissed at first.

However, if we learn to trust these signs, we will usually find that they are indeed angel messages and that they will appear in our lives again and again. We are given subtle signs for a reason; they are a form of gentle intervention to encourage us without alarming us. Often we need these signs during times of stress or heartache and we are usually sent a sign that we can easily cope with.

I have heard of many stories in which a specific butterfly, bird or flower will appear when someone is mourning a loved one or needing comfort. The sign will appear again at the graveside or in the garden when a person feels at their lowest point.

All we have to do is trust, recognise the sign for what it is, and acknowledge the fact that the angels wish to offer us comfort. These lovely little messages can offer us reassurance that all will be well. They can even help to ground us, providing us with a sense of security and support, so that we are then able to move on.

An angel sign is a wonderful gift. Even the darkest cloud has a silver lining – an old but true cliché. Make this moment one of determination to press forwards, in the knowledge that you are never alone and that you can and indeed will be happy once more.

When you make the effort to pay attention to the sights, sounds, smells and sensations around you, you're encouraging yourself to live in the present moment.

DEEPAK CHOPRA MD

Global Connections

There are times when synchronicity leaves us in no doubt that there has to be an inner angel at work in our lives. The expressions 'What are the chances of that happening?' or 'It was meant to be' suggest that, deep down inside, we realise that a spiritual force has brought about extraordinary events. One lady and her family were so astonished by synchronicity that all they could do was marvel at the way things turned out. This is Sylvia's incredible story.

There are numerous reasons why anybody would put up their baby for adoption but one underlying motive is usually the belief that the adopted child will have a better life than the birth parent would be able to provide for it. The overriding concern is for the welfare of the child, although this doesn't necessarily alleviate the pain involved in making the decision.

Today, it's normal for people to have children out of wedlock and there's no stigma attached to either the child or mother. However, this was certainly not always the case and a great deal of pressure was once put on unmarried mothers to give up their babies for adoption. More often than not, the mother was a mere child herself and judged to be unable to cope with a little baby.

Certainly this was the case for Sylvia's mother, who submitted Sylvia for adoption when she was only a few weeks old. Sylvia was raised in a loving and happy environment, and it was only when she was in her middle years that the thought of searching for her biological mother occurred to her.

With today's technology and many agencies willing to help in the search, Sylvia traced her birth mother without too much difficulty. However, it came as a surprise when she found out that her mother had lived in Australia for over thirty years. The geographical distance would be yet another challenge to overcome, but Sylvia rang her mother and they chatted, both delighted to have this contact at last.

They bonded instantly and Sylvia discovered that her mother had thought about her constantly, remembering her birthdays and thinking about her especially at such festive times. Sylvia also learned that her mother had married in Australia and had a grown-up son.

The phone calls between them continued for some time. They eventually decided that they would make every endeavour to meet and so a date was set. It became clear at this point, however, that Sylvia's mother was becoming increasingly frail and was about to move into a care home. So Sylvia and her entire family flew out to Australia. They were aware that Sylvia's mother was by now quite poorly and they were anxious to meet her. Landing in Sydney, they awaited a connecting flight to Adelaide. The old lady lived by the sea in a resort some distance from the city so they knew that there was still quite a long journey ahead of them.

Fate dealt a cruel blow: only a day away from the reunion, Sylvia's mother died. The family felt very sad to have travelled all that way to see her, only to attend her funeral. However, Sylvia did meet her half-brother and they became firm friends. She was also able to see where her mother had lived and learned a great deal more about her and her life.

Determined to look on the bright side, Sylvia arrived back in England content in the knowledge that they had been in contact and that they had chatted away on the phone like old friends for some time before her mother's death. She had also seen where her mother had lived and now she felt closer to her than ever.

Some time later, the story took another dramatic turn when Sylvia was contacted again by the agency that had initially found her mother. To her astonishment, she discovered that she also had a biological brother, who was two years her junior and who had also been given up for adoption. His name, she was told, was David and he was married with a family of his own.

When further details were available, it emerged that David

now lived in Adelaide! He had emigrated there some twenty-five years previously. Amazed, yet 'knowing' deep inside that this coincidence was somehow inevitable, Sylvia decided to ring David. They had a wonderful conversation over the phone. Sylvia told him about their birth mother and the fact that she and her family had travelled to Adelaide just before the old lady's death.

It transpired that David had never made any attempt to trace his mother, and had no idea that she had once lived so near to him. It came as quite a shock to discover that she had lived in the same city on the other side of the world. Everyone, however, was even more astonished when addresses were exchanged and they discovered that David had lived only a few miles from his mother for the past twenty-five years – without having had an idea she was there!

Their mother had lived in a small seaside community outside Adelaide. David explained that he had spent a lot of time in that very spot, taking his children to the beach. It was most extraordinary. He had to conclude that he and his mother must have passed each other often in the street, without ever realising it.

At the time of writing, the brother and sister have not yet met, but they plan to do so one day soon. Here's a true synchronicity of the soul that seems destined to continue into the future.

Connect with someone special.
A loved one is a gift to treasure.

Cheryl Richardson

Small Angels

Angels can be found in the most unusual places; in fact, nowhere on earth is completely angel-free. That said, although we might expect to encounter an angelic presence in a gothic monastery or village church, perhaps a flesh-and-blood angel in a public house is a little out of the ordinary!

It is said that the angels will often send people to step in gently on their behalf when necessary. Certainly this proved to be the case for Deena, who was going through a very difficult time in many respects. Her father was also seriously ill and he was uppermost in her thoughts that particular day, when she went with a friend to a local pub for a cheering drink.

There was live music playing in the pub that lunchtime, which Deena hoped would help to raise her spirits. At one point during a break one of the musicians approached Deena to chat. She thought this very brave of him, considering her non-receptive attitude to admirers at that point! However, the man was very sweet and obviously a nice empathic sort of chap. After a little while, he was asked to play again and, taking his leave, he picked up his guitar.

What happened next was quite extraordinary: the man began to sing song after song that held great significance for Deena. The songs transported her back to her teenage years, to times when she had been blissfully happy. The strange thing was that these were fairly obscure songs, unfamiliar to many of the people listening. It struck Deena as odd that each one should be so unusual yet also particularly meaningful for her.

Signs and symbols have always been very important for Deena and, after the first song, she found herself saying out loud, 'Small angels!' The songs sung by the young man felt like a small sign from these heavenly beings.

Arriving home, Deena felt moved to write a piece of poetry. Although she had felt so low on arriving at the pub, the gentle musician and the significant songs had lifted her mood and now she felt inspired. Her poem ended with the line, 'Maybe some small angel stopped on by to save me'.

Later that day, there was a glorious sunset and Deena found herself still feeling surprisingly mellow. She pottered about and lit the candles in her lounge. The soft candlelight complemented her mood perfectly.

Relaxed and grateful for such a lovely end to the afternoon, Deena went through to the kitchen to make dinner. While she was happily preparing the ingredients, Deena was suddenly filled by a strange sensation – an overwhelming urge to go back into the lounge immediately. Obeying this inner momentum, she rushed through the door, where a frightening sight met her eyes.

When lighting her candles, Deena had placed one of them in a large glass bowl in the centre of the room. The candle must have burned down completely, but not before setting light to the dried potpourri that surrounded it. Now flames were shooting into the air. Carefully grabbing the bowl and rushing to the kitchen, Deena poured water into it. She knew for certain that, had she not gone back into the room at that precise moment, disaster would have occurred. Again, she was convinced that her soul angel had been at work, telling her with its inner voice that danger was near.

When the flames had been extinguished, Deena emptied the burned potpourri from the large bowl. Suddenly she felt something hard at the bottom of the bowl and, to her amazement, lifted out a small crystal angel! She had completely forgotten about this little angel as it had been a gift that had arrived with a broken wing. Feeling sad about it, yet unable to throw the gift away, Deena had glued the wing back in place and forgotten about it. Somehow it had found its way into the glass bowl.

All the signs of the day made a huge impact on Deena. She thought about the gentle musician who had played such significant songs, then her spontaneous exclamation 'small angels!' and her poem about a small angel stopping by to save her.

Deena believes there can be no doubting the message: her angels are simply the blink of an eye away. By the way, the small crystal angel now enjoys a prominent place on her mantelpiece, for all to see!

~ AFFIRMATION ~

I always endeavour to notice even the smallest angel.

Angel in the Shadows

After what felt like a tightrope act, balancing on one leg, Joan faced the daunting task of carrying her cup of tea into the lounge. On a normal daily basis this would be a doddle but, as she lurched through the doorway on her two crutches, getting anywhere without further mishap seemed like a minor miracle. With great difficulty and a little ingenuity, Joan managed to set her cup down on the coffee table and sink with a bump into her comfortable armchair.

'Why me and why now?' she mused, feeling very sorry for herself. It had been such a ridiculously simple accident. Had she sustained a fracture skiing in a glamorous resort or climbing a famous mountain, at least there would have been a little cachet to the whole incident. Sadly, Joan thought, people would only laugh when she told them she had slipped on wet leaves.

Sipping her tea, she glanced through the window into the garden. It was a beautiful autumn day and the sun streamed through the window. However, the beauty was lost on Joan in such a black mood. Mulling over her situation, she realised that she would miss several important meetings at work, not to mention several social events that she had been looking forward too – it was all so upsetting.

She had, of course, many supportive relatives and friends to help her out. In fact, her sister would be along later in the morning to make her lunch, but Joan was not in the mood for counting her blessings!

The morning wore on and Joan's mood became darker; her arms ached from using the crutches and she felt such frustration at not being able to move about with ease. Unexpectedly, a little thought popped into her head, urging her to be calm and to meditate. In retrospect, Joan wondered if the suggestion was perhaps sent to her by an angel.

Angel or not, it was certainly a good idea. In fact, for several years Joan had intermittently attended a meditation group and she had always found meditation helpful. Settling herself now as best she could, she closed her eyes, slowed her breathing and tried to relax. She then recalled one of the guided meditations she had enjoyed so much and concentrated on the imagery.

A lovely calm descended, enveloping Joan and pervading the room. Slowly she opened her eyes and saw an incredible sight: there, on the wall facing her, was the perfect shadow of an angel! The angel was in profile, with its wings folded behind it. Glancing around, Joan could see that the sun streaming through the window had thrown the shadows of the ornaments on the sill against the wall. These ornament shadows made a perfect angel's shape.

At once Joan felt uplifted; the wonderful shadow angel had somehow touched her soul. The incident helped her to realise that the situation she found herself in was only temporary; that she must simply be a little patient and all would soon be well again. There were many people, she reasoned, for whom struggling about on crutches was a daily feature of their lives. She was actually very fortunate and should really count her blessings.

Feeling at once more cheerful about her lot in life, Joan was in a sunny mood by the time her sister arrived. Later in the day, she began to think in depth about the shadow angel and realised that the ornaments had been in place on the windowsill for many years. There had been many sunny days but never before had she spotted a full-length shadow angel! It was a perhaps a sign. Although it was easily explained by natural elements, the timing had been perfect and the impact on Joan's spirit – and indeed soul – was truly remarkable.

This was indeed a case of an angelic sign that could so easily have been missed but that made a huge difference when it was noticed and reflected upon.

Life is mostly froth and bubble,

Two things stand like stone,

Kindness in another's trouble,

Courage in your own.

ADAM LINDSAY GORDON

Soul Token

Choose a pebble or a shell and hold it in the palm of your hand. Sit comfortably and take some deep breaths.

Closing your eyes, visualise a woodland scene emerging in front of you. There is a clearing in the trees and you know instinctively that you are invited to step inside it. Softly, a beautiful reindeer with magnificent antlers also enters the clearing. The reindeer is pulling a light sleigh, which comes to a stop before you. Step into the sleigh and lie back in the comfort of the furs placed there.

Gently, the reindeer pulls away from the clearing and you slowly glide through the forest. It is green and sunny and welcoming and the happiness you feel is all-enveloping. Hills and valleys pass until you pull up alongside a flowing stream, where the water is crystal-clear and makes little gurgling sounds as it passes over the stones. Leaning over the side of the sleigh, you peer into the stream. The stream bed is a treasure trove of stones and shells exactly like the one you hold in your hand. Concentrate on this talisman. How does it feel in your hand? What is its size and texture? Record these facts in your mind.

The sun is beginning to set in the clear sky and shades of turquoise, apricot and gold fill your line of vision. Slowly, the reindeer moves again and pulls you back the way you came through the valleys, hills and forest. The sheer beauty of the sunset takes your breath away and within its layers of colour you can see little angels with sun-dappled wings.

The sleigh reaches the clearing once more and the reindeer stops, allowing you to alight. Step from the sleigh as the light begins to fade but hold on to your talisman.

Take several deep breaths and become aware once more of the room and chair in which you sit. Open your eyes and stretch.

Look carefully at your stone or shell in the palm of your hand. Remember the magical place that the reindeer took you to and the coloured angels in the sky. Every time you hold your token you will remember the beauty of that place and know the angels are watching over you, wherever you may travel.

Leave your burden by the stream,

Life is too short to never dream,

Leave your worries on the shore,

And make the shells your treasure store.

SARAH GARRET-JONES

The Size of the Matter

'Drop two dress sizes in a month', 'Lose that post-pregnancy bulge', 'Fit into those jeans'...on and on it went. I realised that the magazine I had bought was almost exclusively dedicated to issues concerning weight loss. It was full of pictures of celebrities in glamorous dresses and the accompanying captions explained how much weight these women had lost in order to fit into their designer gowns. It was all quite depressing. The message seemed clear: only those people who were a size eight or under were worthy!

Soon after this depressing incident, I noticed a spate of television programmes about people who weighed phenomenal amounts – as much as fifty stone in some cases. These poor individuals couldn't even get out of bed by themselves and were struggling mentally and emotionally, as well as physically, to come to terms with their condition. Often they would resort to surgery for help.

In my mind, the two extremes sat side by side – ultra-thin set against ultra-heavy. It seemed to me that the West may have everything it desires in terms of food but that this is also causing us some serious mental and physical problems. Tracey discovered this contradiction all too painfully for herself.

All at Sea

The cruise was to be the trip of a lifetime. Family and close friends were joining Tracey on the voyage to celebrate her thirtieth birthday, and now she stepped excitedly aboard. One niggling doubt remained, however, and it concerned her wardrobe: how could she ever look glamorous next to so many slim and elegant people? Weight had always been a problem for Tracey, causing her considerable heartache over the years.

From her mid-teens onwards her weight had steadily increased. Her sedentary job and robust appetite had not helped, and the fact that she had no enthusiasm for sport or for exercise of any kind merely compounded the situation. Every New Year her resolution was the same – 'this year I shall lose weight!' – and joining slimming clubs had become an annual ritual.

Here she was, embarking on a wonderful holiday with a suitcase full of clothes designed mainly to cover up, rather than emphasise, her figure. Her family had planned this trip as a surprise and, while Tracey loved them for their thoughtfulness, nevertheless she was full of foreboding.

In the event, it proved to be a wonderful holiday. Everyone loved the locations, the sunshine and especially the food – of which there appeared to be an endless supply. Towards the end of the voyage, Tracey began to feel miserable, but she tried hard to hide the fact. Her clothes, which had been designed to be loose and comfortable, were now straining at the seams! To top it all, the ship was full of so many elegant ladies that Tracey couldn't stop herself from feeling inferior. Keeping a cheerful face, she nevertheless thanked her family profusely for the lovely holiday and assured them it had made her very happy.

When she arrived home alone to her little flat, Tracey found herself in tears. Sobbing into her pillow that night, she simply didn't know what she could do to achieve her goal of losing weight. Later, she still couldn't sleep, so she went into the kitchen to make a cup of tea. Out of the corner of her eye, she spotted an angel card that she had pinned on her kitchen notice board after attending a workshop.

Taking the card down, she began to think about all she had heard and read about angels. She had been told that they were always ready to help in any way they could. Was it possible that they would help her with this pressing problem?

Sensible enough when feeling rational, Tracey knew in her heart that she was a talented, loving and worthy person, but she also knew that her health and happiness were at risk. She had gained so much weight on her holiday and, as far as she could tell, the problem would only get worse. Holding the angel card, she closed her eyes and asked fervently for the angels to help her.

She slowly felt a glow spread through her, warm and bright and almost defying description. Tracey says, 'It was as if a warm light had been switched on in my soul.' The glow continued to spread until it felt all-encompassing and in that moment Tracey knew her angel had answered. Sensations of strength and support filled her heart and she knew that she had turned the corner. Telling herself she would achieve health and happiness, she was truly convinced her angel would be with her every step of the way.

I would like to report that Tracey's problems immediately came to an end and that she sailed through her efforts to reduce her weight. However, that was not the case: the process took quite some time, lots of determination and willpower. The feelings of support and angelic love, however, never left her. The sensations she experienced that night remain to this day.

Tracey is much happier with her weight today. She feels strong and healthy – and plans to remain that way. She says, 'It was a revelation to me to realise that the angels are there to help in whatever way you need them. Whatever the problem, if you are suffering they will be there for you.'

Your own angel within can help you to lift your soul; you only have to ask.

A woman's life can really be a succession
of lives, each revolving around some
emotionally compelling situation or
challenge, and each marked off
by some intense experience.

WALLIS SIMPSON

Achieving with Your Angel

Your inner angel can help you achieve your dreams. But first you have to know what your dreams are. And your angel will also need you to take some practical steps of your own if she is to support you.

On a piece of paper or in your special Angel Book, note down your answers to the following questions.

* What do you desire most in life?

* What can you do to make this desire a reality?

* Are any negative thoughts holding you back?

* Do you feel love for yourself?

* Do you worry about what others may think of you?

Now concentrate on the following points and know that each one of them is true.

* Your angel loves you unconditionally.

* Your angel has every faith in you.

* Whatever your problem your angel can help.

* Your heart's desire may be achieved if you trust.

* If you promise yourself to be positive, all will be well
  – whatever the outcome.

Finally, whatever your problems, doubts or worries, ask your angel to come into your life and give you guidance. Look for avenues and directions to go down in order to achieve your goals.

AFFIRMATION

*I will put complete trust
in my angel.*

Lonely Hearts

Living alone can be very difficult, with some people finding it more of a challenge than others. It had been six years since Faye and her husband had parted company and, although she felt it had been the right thing to do, she found life by herself often very hard to cope with.

Friends had been kind and had tried to introduce nice men to her, but none of them had clicked. Living in the city of Los Angeles among three and a half million souls, Faye mused that surely there must be someone out there for her! In fact, Los Angeles County had a head count of ten million people, so surely there had to be a suitable companion somewhere!

One beautiful spring morning, Faye picked up a magazine in the supermarket. It was her day off and she was planning to enjoy a lazy couple of hours in the garden, drinking coffee and reading. Arriving home, she put away her groceries, made her coffee and stepped out into the sunny garden with her new magazine. A happy hour went by before Faye eventually reached the magazine's back pages. A particular feature caught her eye: it was a 'Lonely Hearts' column. Reading this column, which listed people searching for partners, Faye found that many of the descriptions sounded very intriguing indeed.

One man described himself so attractively that Faye was sorely tempted to answer his ad on the spot. It was as if this person was reaching out just to her, so vivid was the impression she had of him. Faye was a successful businesswoman, and she prided herself on her good judgement and her strong instinct for choosing the right people to work for her. Now she felt sure that this same strong intuitive sense was leading her to single out this person from the long column of others.

Several days passed and, many hours of pondering later, Faye took her courage into her hands and wrote a letter to the man whose ad had stood out from the crowd. Telling herself she had nothing to lose, she quickly sealed and posted her letter. To her amazement, Faye received a reply from the man almost by return of post.

Calling at her post office box the next morning to collect her mail as she did every day, Faye discovered the letter waiting for her. Lifting it from her box, number 916, she paused to read the postmark, wondering just how far away this person might live. She had herself written to a post office box when contacting him.

Faye's post office box sat with hundreds of others in a long corridor of featureless, grey metal containers. As she stared at the handwritten envelope, she was suddenly aware that someone was watching her and, looking up, noticed a very handsome man peering over her shoulder. To her surprise, he began to laugh out loud as she looked on, totally puzzled.

After a second or two, he explained with a twinkle that the letter she was holding in her hand had been sent by him! It turned out that his post office box was number 917 – right next to hers!

Faye then laughed too, and they agreed that the chances of them having adjacent boxes, or indeed living in the same district in a city that was so vast, were astonishing. Chatting happily about the wonderful synchronicity, they realised that any ice between them had been well and truly broken, and they cheerfully went to a local coffee shop together for a drink and further chat.

As you might have predicted, this meeting was to be the first of many and blossomed into a fulfilling relationship. Faye's friends have been known to tease her about 'male order', but she corrects them with a knowing smile as she replies, 'Angel mail order!'

A guardian angel o'er his life presiding,

Doubling his pleasures, and his cares dividing.

SAMUEL ROGERS

Soul Mates

Most of us will be familiar with the expression 'soul mate' and perhaps many of us will have longed to meet a soul mate of our own. Do we all – as the saying goes – have one out there somewhere? We may have partners with whom we live in perfect harmony and happily coexist throughout our lives, but how can we tell if they our magical soul mates?

To answer these age-old questions, I am drawn to the work of the eighteenth-century theologian Emanuel Swedenborg, whose writings I often refer to in my books and whose knowledge about the instructions of angels remains, in my view, unparalleled. Swedenborg tells us that angels communicated with him on a daily basis over a period of twenty-five years, and that he wrote down the wisdom they imparted. He says that the person we spend our lives with on earth may be, but is not necessarily, our soul mate. He adds that that we will certainly find our soul mate in the next life, as we will all have a soul mate in heaven. It is an interesting thought and a rather lovely one, whether or not we choose to believe it.

Yet what proportion of people are fortunate enough to find these special partners on earth and how can we recognise them if we do?

A friend of mine, happily married for many years, was attending a business conference one week. Finding herself momentarily alone during a break on the first day, she took her cup of coffee out onto a balcony. There she came across a man who was also drinking his coffee. He turned to greet her with a smile.

She tells me it was as if the sun had begun to shine in her soul, so strong was the sensation she felt. As she talked to the man, she was astonished to discover that there were many connections between them, and the pair of them chatted as if they had known each other all their lives. 'Never before have I experienced such a connection with another human,' said my friend. 'It was uncanny.'

When the conference came to an end several days later, they said goodbye. 'It was so surreal,' she told me later. 'It was as if I was leaving part of me behind.'

Both of them were fortunate to have happy marriages and neither of them would ever put their family's harmony in jeopardy, but they each knew that their soul connection would always be there.

Several years passed and there have been many strange incidents in their lives. Travelling on a train one day, a year after the encounter, my friend was thinking about this man when he unexpectedly climbed aboard at the next stop. This was in an unfamiliar city and, when he spotted her, he revealed that she had been on his mind since the first thing that morning.

On another occasion, the man misdialled a mobile phone number and found he had reached my friend. Both of them were astonished because they had not exchanged their phone numbers.

It is as if this deep connection will not go away and so the universe arranges for them to meet and from time to time to ensure they have contact. These soul coincidences continue sporadically years after their first meeting and my friend says she totally believes Swedenborg's teaching on the subject and that she feels sure she and her soul mate will be together in the next life.

Soul mates may not necessarily be of a romantic nature at all, as some same-sex friends may bond and feel so alike that their relationship becomes comfortable and lifelong. A friend may understand exactly what you need to get across, will be most understanding in all aspects of your life and a delight to share happy occasions and news with. Such a friend may be the first person you turn to on hearing important or emotional news, and you love and respect that person unconditionally. They are rare individuals and, if you are lucky enough to have one, cherish that friend.

Sometimes even a grandchild may be a soul mate. The bond between the older and younger generations can be very strong and special.

One thing is for certain ~ that we often feel a connection with others which words alone cannot explain. It is something that comes from deep inside, is one of life's great blessings and links our very souls.

Angels guide us to become spiritual people
for the pleasure of it,

Not for its moralism, for the spiritual life itself

Has a great deal of beauty and real
satisfaction, even pleasure,

And this is what the soul needs.

THOMAS MOORE

Warm on a Winter's Day

A beautiful snowy winter's day creates a perfect opportunity for admiring nature and a spot of meditation. If you feel up to it, wrap yourself up well and go for a walk, preferably to a quiet place. Should you live in the country, take a walk down a lane, or, if you are a city dweller, perhaps you can find a local park.

I have actually tried this simple visualisation when sitting by the window in a busy city coffee bar, but it needed a little more imagination than usual! To try it yourself, a winter setting is ideal. First reach a sense of calm by breathing slowly and steadily for a few moments.

Concentrate on the falling snowflakes, picturing their wonderful individual patterns in your mind's eye. See in each of their forms the snowflake star with its many graceful strands and branches. Although each flake has a unique pattern, all are equally beautiful.

Now imagine seeing right inside each snowflake: there is a tiny angel, floating to earth with the intention of touching a person walking below. Each flake that alights on a head, shoulder or arm imparts a blessing.

As you feel the little snowflakes land and melt on your body, turn your face upwards and feel them on your skin. Each flake is the kiss of an angel and your very own blessing. Give thanks for the wonder of nature.

An angel, robed in spotless white

Bent down and kissed the sleeping Night,

Night woke to blush: the sprite was gone,

Men saw the blush and called it dawn.

PAUL LAURENCE DUNBAR

Homeward Bound

This is the amazing story of how a book finally found its way home. It was as though each person connected with this volume was inspired, when the time was right, to start a chain reaction – or perhaps a 'soul train'. It is almost as if the angels said, 'Right, everybody – act now!'

The story begins over three hundred years ago, when the book in question was written by Emanuel Swedenborg, the Swedish mystic and theologian. The book was originally written in Latin and entitled *Arcana Caelestia*. It was eventually translated into English by scholars at the Swedenborg Society in London. The society was set up in 1810 and still exists today, based in Bloomsbury Way in the capital.

The society's first copy of the English edition of *Arcana Caelestia* appears to have disappeared into a black hole for many years before resurfacing at the home of my friend Veronica Williams in Glossop, Derbyshire. She told me how it came to be in her possession.

Veronica's son arrived home one day in the early 1990s with a box of books. He explained that his friend was emigrating to a new life in Africa and was giving away to friends items he could not take with him. Searching through the box, Veronica's son came across the volume of *Arcana Caelestia* and immediately gave it to his mother, saying he felt it was more 'her sort of thing'. Indeed, Veronica is interested in all things of a spiritual nature.

She saw that the book had been printed in Manchester more than one hundred years ago and that the cover was distinctly the worse for wear. However, when she sat down to read it, the dense nature of the book defeated her and it eventually found its way onto a shelf, where it was destined to stay for some fifteen years.

As the years rolled by, Veronica thought about the book from time to time, aware that it really belonged in a library or appropriate collection. However, she was unsure exactly where that might be.

By coincidence, Veronica was working as an alternative therapist and had occasion to be in New Church College, Manchester at the time I was working there. Meeting at that time, we found we had a happy connection because Veronica had in fact read some of my books. We met again at one of my workshops in North Wales.

Eventually we discussed her copy of *Arcana Caelestia* but no action was taken at that point; clearly, the time was still not right. Eventually, however, having decided to de-clutter her home in a spring clean, Veronica felt inspired to pass the book on to me. After careful consideration, I decided the rightful place for this very old and precious work would be the Swedenborg Society in London and so I duly parcelled it up and posted it off to them by registered post.

On the inside of the book was the original owner's signature – a Dr Henry Bateman – and an address in Islington, London. I wondered if the people at the Society might have some information about this man.

Again, by another extraordinary stroke of luck, at the same time that the book arrived at its destination in Bloomsbury, the Society Secretary, Richard Lyons, received a letter from South Africa. It was from Philip Bateman, who was researching his family tree. In his letter, he explained that his great-grandfather had been involved with the Swedenborgian Church and he wondered if the Society happened to have any information about him!

It was a truly amazing coincidence: the book had been languishing all those years on a shelf and at the very time that Veronica felt moved to pass it on, a relative of the past owner got in touch with the Swedenborg Society.

The book was duly parcelled up once more and sent this time to Philip in South Africa. Delighted with this lovely old work, Philip sent a wonderful thank you letter and generous donation to the Society. He has since had the book recovered and it is one of his prized possessions. The story is a clear case of spiritual synchronicity at work once more.

Further research revealed that Dr Henry Bateman was in fact a distinguished Senior Surgeon at the London Cholera Hospital. He became a convert to the Swedenborgian religion and worked tirelessly as a social reformer, giving free medical advice to anyone in need who approached him. He was also instrumental in founding various educational establishments for young people. He would surely be astonished to learn how widely travelled his book has been – and how happy to realise that it finally found its way home!

Soul-full

We can all start a 'soul train' of our own by activating the powers of our inner angel. If we radiate the feelings and truths that our inner angel helps us uncover, we will set events in motion.

We can begin by paying attention to events such as coincidences and pondering their meaning. This will lead us to the next step and we will begin to make sense of the direction in which events are leading us.

Likewise, if we notice and acknowledge the angel signs that surround us in nature, the angels will respond by ensuring that their signs become more frequent and explicit in our lives.

A friend once told me that when you want
something badly and it does not happen,
there is usually a good reason. For the right
decisions the right time will always come.

DANIEL BARENBOIM

A Guide for Life

I have a good friend who possesses a gift that she has difficulty classifying. I think most people would call her clairvoyant, but her gift appears to be much more at times than that word would suggest. Her predictions are incredibly accurate and her visionary guidance is much sought-after. However, one aspect of her work she cannot predict is that of timing. Although she may be confident that an encounter will occur or an opportunity arise, she cannot predict exactly when this will happen.

The issue of timing is also true of many spiritual encounters: we may be given a sign that angels are there to help us, but the actual angelic help may not manifest itself in our lives for some time to come. Jane certainly found this to be the case.

At the age of twenty, Jane had to enter hospital for an operation to remove her wisdom teeth. During the procedure there seem to have been complications relating to the anaesthetic and Jane found herself undergoing what is typically referred to as a 'near-death experience'. She became aware of a tunnel opening up in front of her, an extremely bright light and a figure emerging from the light.

To Jane's delight, the figure was that of her grandmother, whom she called Nana. She had enjoyed a very close relationship with her nana, who had passed away the previous year. Behind her nana, Jane could see many other figures, appearing as if in a mist.

At this point a very distinct voice said firmly to her: 'You must go back. This is not your time; there are many things yet for you to do.'

Later, when her surgeon talked her through what had

happened, she realised just how dangerous the situation had been. The surgeon explained that she had experienced great trouble breathing during the operation and that the staff had worked hard to stabilise her. Hearing what he said, Jane and her mother exchanged knowing glances. Clearly, Jane had been returned for a reason.

Indeed, she would be needed in the future, as her nana had predicted. Many serious physical challenges lay ahead for Jane, during which it became clear to her that the angels had a plan for her.

Living in Sydney, Australia, with her husband and grown-up son years later, Jane was extremely happy. It was therefore a bittersweet situation when her husband declared that a great job opportunity had arisen for him in another state, which would involve the two of them moving, and leaving their son behind. The family would of course stay closely in touch and Jane felt she had to give her husband the chance to follow his dream.

Shortly after the move, however, things began to take a turn for the worse. Jane's husband became seriously ill and tests revealed that he needed a liver transplant. Jane's heart sank, as she knew only too well how long the waiting list can be for a transplant organ to become available. However, to their astonishment, a donor organ was found within only two weeks – something that would never have happened had they stayed in Sydney. It was at this point that Jane realised the angels were helping her to make good decisions and that they were looking after both her and her husband.

This angelic guidance continued throughout the coming years, especially during the difficult times when Jane's mother faced serious illness. This situation culminated when her mother was dying. At the same time, her husband was once more undergoing crucial surgery. Jane found herself torn between the two people she loved, emotionally and physically.

However, dreadful though it was, there was a real blessing in this situation. The nurse who was looking after Jane's mother was a close relative of them both and one evening Jane received a phone call from this dear lady, Cheryl, to say that her mother was very close to death. Cheryl held the phone close to Jane's mother's ear, and they were able to speak to each other at this crucial time, telling each other of their love. It was a very special experience and yet Jane was able to stay by her husband's bedside throughout it.

Shortly after the phone call, Jane walked past an open window and felt a distinctly cool breeze touch her face. She knew instinctively that her mother had passed away that moment. The clock told her it was 11.05 p.m.

At the same time, Cheryl noticed an expression on Jane's mother's face that she had seen many times before in her capacity as a nurse. Jane's mother was staring intently at the ceiling, seeing something or someone that no one else could. Turning to Cheryl and her son, Jane's brother, who was also at her bedside, she told them that her time had come, that she loved them and then she simply said, 'Goodbye.'

Many difficult tasks lay ahead for Jane. She was still very worried about her husband and yet she had to help to arrange her mother's funeral. And she knew that it would involve some clever timing and support from the angels for her even to attend the funeral.

However, it seems to Jane that in the event the angels helped her through these and many other challenging situations in her life. She has indeed had a lot to do in looking after her family, and it is clear to her now why she had to recover from her near-death experience all those years ago. Then, the angels touched her soul and they have guided her from that moment on.

Angels are pointing to what we call God…
And this ocean of love is us and we come
from it and we go back to it, and all the cells
in our bodies are composed of it.

SOPHIE BURNHAM

* ✳ *

Firing in All Senses

Throughout this book, we have taken an in-depth look at the role of our physical senses in angelic interventions. Looking at the evidence, it seems clear that all five of our senses can come into play whenever angels are around. Moreover, there is strong evidence that the 'sixth sense' or 'inner angel' is a vital aspect of angelic communication for many people.

There is one question that occurs to me, however: are there any angel experiences that involve all the senses at the same time? My research suggests that the answer is a resounding 'yes'! Although such an overload of the senses is incredibly rare, there are examples of exactly these kinds of angelic experience.

I have always been of the opinion that each individual receives whatever they can cope with whenever the angels are involved, and that the angels will give us the appropriate spiritual response for our specific situation. This means that dramatic situations will receive dramatic responses. The sight of a huge, shining angel occurs most often when a person is in urgent need of help. Usually that person will be seriously distressed or facing danger.

On the other hand, a gentle intervention happens most often when a person simply needs to be reminded that he or she is not alone and an angel is close. This may be in the form of a symbol, either from nature, music or another medium, which offers reassurance when times are a little difficult.

By definition, if a person has all his or her senses activated in an angel encounter, this would lead us to believe that the situation itself needed the strongest form of angelic intervention. This was certainly true in the case of Elaine, when the angels helped to turn a dramatic episode in her life into one of peace and goodwill.

Enveloped by Angels

For Elaine, the sense of gloom was all-pervading. No single thought or feeling could bring a chink of light into her life, so awful was her situation.

The first event in a cascade of misfortune came when she received the result of recent medical tests and learned that she had cancer. Although the prognosis was uncertain, it seemed that the cancer was inoperable. Elaine had to gather herself together simply to comprehend this news.

Sadly, her marriage, which had been shaky for some time, now appeared to be unravelling. Her husband was quite an introverted man who found it difficult to discuss their problems; his chosen method of dealing with them was simply to bury his head in the sand in the hope that they would go away. Elaine desperately wanted to talk to him but was met with a wall of silence.

Teaching had been Elaine's chosen profession and the love of her life. Children always cheered her, their enthusiasm rubbing off on her and making her feel uplifted. Not now, however – she could not face the classroom with its bustling noise. Nor could she cope with the staff room, where the thought of having to share such personal news filled her with horror.

Overwhelmed by her sense of isolation, she fell into a deep state of depression. Although she knew she was being treated kindly and caringly by the staff at her medical consultations, she could not help feeling that really she was just another patient statistic. Each day became more difficult than the last and she retreated from friends and neighbours as she sank deeper into fear and grief.

One morning when she woke up alone, her husband having been away for a couple of days on a business trip, Elaine felt lower than she could ever recall having done in her life. Calls home from her husband had seemed rather sharp and perfunctory; clearly he was still avoiding the sensitive subject altogether. As she sat in bed, the day stretched ahead of her in utter misery and despair.

With a sharp flash of realisation, Elaine saw the solution. The only way out of all of this was to bring life itself to an end. Swiftly she got dressed, rushed downstairs and grabbed her car keys, determined to put her suffering to an end immediately.

It was still early morning and the surrounding country lanes were very quiet. Driving towards the hills in the distance, she formulated a plan in her mind. The road would soon become very steep and, on reaching the brow of a familiar hill, she would simply drive at full speed off the top – plunging to the valley floor and ending her life.

Agitated but determined, she drove at speed until she reached the steep incline that led to the summit of the hill. As she had expected, there was virtually no traffic and she approached the crest of the hill to find the road ahead clear. On the very brow of the hill she stopped the car. Looking down at the steep sides of the road, she knew that to go over the edge here at speed would be certain death, but at that particular moment it was all she craved.

After a short silent prayer to God and his angels, Elaine was ready to re-start the engine and take action. In that instant, however, the interior of the car filled with a bright, intense light and Elaine caught her breath. Tingling sensations rippled through her entire body and the distinct sensation of a hand being placed gently on the top of her head made her still and silent. A voice said softly, 'Go back. Help is there.'

Suddenly, the light within the car took the shape of a figure. Elaine knew for certain that this was an angel who had heard her prayers. Waves of love surrounded her and peace at last filled her mind.

Once the vision had gone, Elaine sat for some time in a daze, collecting her thoughts and feelings. She carefully turned the car around to head home.

Arriving home she walked into her kitchen, trembling but full of wonder that the angels had chosen to help her at the very moment she needed them most. Almost automatically, she switched on the kettle to make herself a strong cup of tea, wondering how long it would take her to fully absorb what had just happened.

Having poured the scalding water into the teapot, she took off her coat and went to hang it up in the hall. As she did so, a figure appeared through the glass panel in the front door. It was one of her colleagues from work.

Elaine opened the door and asked her teacher friend to come in and have a cup of tea with her. Her colleague had brought her a bag full of get well cards from staff and pupils, as well as many drawings from the children, and in her hand she balanced a delicious chocolate cake that was the perfect accompaniment to tea!

Tears fell down Elaine's cheeks as she hugged her friend. Clearly, everyone did care and she felt the glow of love shared. For the first time, Elaine talked about her problems and her lovely colleague listened. It was exactly what was needed: a sympathetic ear and a gesture of caring.

Eating the delicious cake, Elaine said, 'This is indeed angel cake,' and nothing had ever tasted so good.

This happened several years ago. Elaine faced the surgery and her treatment had a happy outcome, even though it came after many chemotherapy sessions. Her husband stood by her and eventually the crisis brought them closer. Back teaching full-time, Elaine constantly gives thanks to God and his angels for their intervention on that dreadful day.

'Life is precious,' she says. And it's wonderful that she was given the chance to live it to the full.

> *The feeling of being loved and supported by the Universe in general and by certain recognisable spirits in particular is bliss.*
>
> ALICE WALKER

Making Sense

When the situation demands, help in the form of enveloping love is received. All manner of angelic interventions can be received according to the requirements of the situation. However, what if the crisis involves a person who is almost totally deprived of the means to perceive the angels through the usual physical senses of sight, touch, hearing, smell and taste? How does communication succeed in such a case, firstly with another human soul, never mind with the angels?

The incredibly brave Helen Keller created a unique record of what it means to live in such circumstances. The full details of her situation still leave me breathless with admiration. Fate dealt a blow to Helen that would have crushed other mortals, yet her indomitable spirit shone through her trials and tribulations.

Helen was born a perfectly healthy baby on 27 June 1880 in Alabama, USA. However, before she was two years old she had contracted a severe condition named only as 'brain fever' by the doctors of the time. The precise nature of the illness remains a mystery to this day. It became apparent that the illness had left Helen without sight or hearing, in effect rendering her dumb, as she had not yet learned to speak. Her parents were left wondering how on earth anyone could reach her in such a state of isolation.

Despite this, her spirit shone through and a miracle occurred one day when her teacher had a brilliant idea. Anne Sullivan had been filling a mug with cold water one day from a pump outdoors, when she was inspired to hold Helen's hand under the cold water and then spell out the word 'water' on Helen's hand with her finger. The shock of the cold water and a repeated tracing of the word got through to Helen, and soon other words were traced and understood by her. It was a monumental breakthrough into Helen's isolated world.

Helen grew to be deeply spiritual and followed the teachings of Emanuel Swedenborg. She even wrote books herself, most notably her autobiography *Light in My Darkness*, a very special book indeed. Her sensual deprivation could not keep the spiritual aspects of her being from flourishing.

It is almost beyond belief to imagine a person surviving without the everyday senses that most of us take for granted and are fortunate enough to enjoy. Helen certainly had an angel within her soul who guided her throughout her life.

*I cannot understand why anyone should
fear death – life divides and estranges,
while that which at heart is life eternal,
reunites and reconciles.*

HELEN KELLER

How to Be a Happy Soul!

The ways in which inner harmony and peace touch our soul will
be experienced differently by each of us. To my surprise, I have
found that scenery which I find very beautiful will not appeal to
everyone. I have a very practical friend who, when I pointed out
a particularly wonderful sunset, explained in great detail that it
was merely the effect of dirt particles in the air! Similarly, the
effects of beautiful music may be lost on some people, but if we
remain unmoved by some things then there will be other
aspects of life that will reach our souls.

I believe that we each have to exercise our own particular
method of 'soul searching'. You may have found there is a
situation that always moves you emotionally and resonates
within your soul, such as walking along a winter beach, listening
to the voice of someone you love or simply drinking a glass of
ice-cold water on a hot day. If so, try to repeat the experience
when you can and let your soul soar.

There are many other experiences that you might try. For

instance, on a clear, cold night, find a place away from street-lights and marvel at the stars. Maybe drive to the top of a hill in your favourite stretch of countryside, park the car and drink in the view. In spring or summer, when the weather forecast reports a fine sunny day to follow, rise early and watch the sunrise in peace and quiet.

There may be some occasions that moved you that would be impossible to recreate. If so, close your eyes and visualise those events, sensing the wonder you felt at the time.

One of the most awe-inspiring events in my own life was when I witnessed the Aurora Borealis in Iceland. I very much doubt I shall ever see the Northern Lights again, but that original sensation of awe is easy for me to recall if I close my eyes and concentrate. Maybe you have been fortunate enough to witness this magical sight for yourself; if so, you can always recreate the wonder in meditation.

You may have other memories that move you. Perhaps you once found yourself caught up in the emotions of a crowd of people, singing in unison or cheering a wonderful event? The unity and mutual happiness of a large crowd can produce sheer exhilaration.

Sometimes a solitary pursuit can be a source of happiness. Perhaps you have a talent for painting, pottery or photography that you simply need to refresh? Recall how happy you once felt indulging in these activities and try them once more.

So many different events and activities can touch the soul. Ask your inner angel to guide you to such sources so that you too can experience soul happiness.

What lies behind us
and what lies before us
are tiny matters compared
to what lies
within us.

RALPH WALDO EMERSON

✳ ✳ ✳

Grant to me that I may be made
beautiful in my soul within and that all
external possessions be in harmony
with my inner man.

May I consider the wise man rich,
and may I have such wealth as only the
self-restrained man can bear
or endure.

SOCRATES

Connect with Your Inner Angel

When next visiting your sacred space, I want you to concentrate on your inner angel. Do you have a little statue of an angel or perhaps a picture from a birthday card or Christmas card? Place this angel in front of you and open your mind to the fact that inside your heart there is an angel guiding you throughout life. Whenever you feel moved emotionally by beauty or kindness, this is your soul responding to that inner angel. Know that, if you exercise your angelic qualities, they will increase. Moreover, you will encourage all around you to exercise their angelic qualities too. Focusing on your sacred space, ask your angel to be with you, guiding your journey through life. Be aware of the simple truth that, if you ask, you will receive. Thank your angel for enriching your soul.

A Harmony
of Angels

I sincerely hope that the stories in this book, which have been contributed by people from myriad backgrounds – social, geographical, economic, racial and religious – will have convinced you that angels are there for us all. Communicating with the angels is very much a case of our opening ourselves up to them and allowing them access to our hearts and minds.

I also trust the chapters in this book have shown how all our different senses can be involved when it comes to angelic interventions. We may be deprived of one or more of our vital senses, but the angels can still communicate with us if we allow them to. Not everyone will see an angel; in fact, seeing angels is probably the rarest form of intervention. The medium most suitable to our particular situation may be an encounter in the form of a wonderful fragrance, sound, touch or taste.

Frequently, an angel encounter may be accompanied by doubt. This is chiefly because the ways in which the angels communicate with us can be so subtle that we sometimes fail to recognise them. If, for only a fleeting moment, you find yourself asking, 'Was that really a message from the angels?' then often you will discover later that it was. Trust the sign, no matter how insignificant it may appear, and you will usually find that it will be repeated on another day. To welcome the angels into your life, challenge your scepticism and allow yourself to suspend your disbelief. The more you trust, the more frequent the signs from the angels will become.

One of the best-known signs linked with angels is that of a feather. So many people have told me that the first time they found an unusual white feather they dismissed it as a strange incident and looked for a rational explanation. Could the cat have brought it inside? Was the pristine feather somehow brought into the house on the sole of a shoe? Did it float into the house through an open window, dropped by a passing bird?

This would be their train of thought – even though they knew deep inside that none of these explanations was likely. In my experience, feathers have frequently been found in rooms that had been locked, with windows shut tight. Similarly, the person who found the feather may have never owned a cat. And, finally, surely the feather would be flattened and dirty – not immaculate and fluffy – if it had been stuck to a shoe? Accounts have reached me of people finding white, fluffy feathers outside their homes in the rain, yet the feathers themselves somehow remain dry!

Eventually, in most cases where feathers have been found and those involved have kept an open mind, the conclusion would be reached that this indeed was a gift from the angels. When this was truly believed other feathers would appear, or other angel signs that are equally easy to read.

You do not have to wait for a sign if you want to connect

with your own inner angel. Simply try one of the exercises or meditations earlier in this book. We can all feel the deep sense of angelic peace and love surround us when we meditate on the angels and ask them to come into our life.

Once we invite the angels to come closer to us, they will bring harmony to all aspects of our lives and we in turn can radiate this out to all we come into contact with. With a little angelic inspiration, we are literally capable of starting a peace movement all on our own – and if enough of us join in we could change the world!

The title of this book is, of course, *An Angel to Guide Me*. I hope that, if there was ever any doubt in your mind that you have an angelic guide, this book will have dispelled that doubt. We have seen how other people met with angels, and you will have discovered suggestions in these pages that will help you to contact the angels yourself, encouraging them to show you signs of their love. We all have an angel to guide us; we need only to trust and believe.

I wish you the joy of angels and trust that their blessings will reach you in the most appropriate sense. I hope you will have been inspired and comforted by the many true stories in this book.

May you find angelic harmony in your life,

Glennyce Eckersley

ALSO AVAILABLE FROM RIDER

Order further Rider titles from your local bookshop or have them delivered to your door by Bookpost.

By Glennyce Eckerley:

☐ An Angel at My Shoulder   9781846040658   £6.99

☐ Angels to Watch Over Us   9781846040306   £6.99

☐ Saved by the Angels   9780712612173   £6.99

By Glennyce Eckersley and Gary Quinn:

☐ An Angel Forever   9781844135790   £7.99

☐ Angel Awakenings   9781846040610   £9.99

☐ Angels Believe and Receive   9781846040863   £7.99

FREE POSTAGE AND PACKING
Overseas customers allow £2.00 per paperback

By phone: 01624 677237

By post: Random House Books
c/o Bookpost
PO Box 29, Douglas, Isle of Man, IM99 1BQ

By fax: 01624 670923

By email: bookshop@enterprise.net

Cheques (payable to Bookpost) and credit cards accepted.
Prices and availability subject to change without notice. Allow 28 days for delivery.
When placing your order, please mention if you do not wish to receive any additional information.

www.rbooks.co.uk